Foreword

Appalachia has been the nation's industrial engine since the late nineteenth century. While Appalachia has been synonymous with the coal industry, the region and its people have also been shaped by the extraction and processing of minerals. Collectively, these dangerous industries have helped naturalize the logic of profits over people. This emphasis on profit has also shaped the region's landscape, both physically and socially, leaving behind a legacy of environmental damage and social injustice. Through their activism, in all its forms, Appalachians have consistently sought to build alternatives to the world extractive industries have created, advocating for social justice, environmental protections, fair wages, safe working conditions, and access to health care. Their stories have been a denial of the advancement of corporate greed and the wreckage that extractive capitalism has left at our feet.

Restorative work by historians and activists has broadened interest in infamous events like the 1921 Battle of Blair Mountain and the burdens of early coal miners and their families. As the coal industry accelerated production between 1900 and 1930, Appalachian workers inhabited a world where disaster could strike at any time, leaving them to navigate crises of injury, disability, sickness, or unemployment. Efforts to secure fair wages and safer working conditions could be protracted and sometimes violent. The obstacles, and the losses, were often total in a world where private industry controlled access to housing, food, transportation, schools, and even the political system. The stories of these battles and the workers who waged them have been critical to forming aspects of an Appalachian identity for many who claim both a real and desired heritage of resistance.

By contrast, encounters with stories of Appalachian activism beyond union campaigns and labor unrest are more fleeting. This is not because hostilities lessened but because they shifted from direct confrontation with industry leaders to navigating complex bureaucratic systems. As extractive industries declined after 1950, workers and their families discovered new battles for pensions, health care, disability benefits, and access to new services promised by an array of government antipoverty programs. These programs, while intended to assist, often presented their own challenges with confusing eligibility requirements and lengthy application processes. The fight for these entitlements, benefits, and assistance was less visible than the dramatic strikes and protests of earlier eras. These campaigns were often grassroots and organized by individuals within their communities, and many of the leaders were women. Their efforts, while crucial for the well-being of their families and communities, have been less recognized in historical narratives, partly due to societal biases that undervalued women's contributions and grassroots activism.

In *To Live Here, You Have to Fight,* historian Jessica Wilkerson writes that Appalachian women "tended to the broken bodies of miners, mourned the dead, raised children, fought for clean water, fed the families of striking workers, carried their neighbors to hospitals, helped relatives navigate welfare offices, implemented school lunch programs, distributed educational resources, sheltered abused women and children, fought for parental leave, and much more." These caregiving activities sustained families through times of hardship and sometimes led to systemic change or life-altering victories. Campaigns to improve access to health care were a natural

WE WERE PROMISED

WE WERE PROMISED

HOW AN APPALACHIAN GRANDMOTHER FOUGHT A CORPORATE GIANT

JULIA FLINT

FOREWORD BY ELIZABETH CATTE

Published by The University Press of Kentucky, scholarly publisher for the Commonwealth, serving Bellarmine University, Berea College, Centre College of Kentucky, Eastern Kentucky University, The Filson Historical Society, Georgetown College, Kentucky Historical Society, Kentucky State University, Morehead State University, Murray State University, Northern Kentucky University, Spalding University, Transylvania University, University of Kentucky, University of Louisville, University of Pikeville, and Western Kentucky University.

Editorial and Sales Offices: The University Press of Kentucky
663 South Limestone Street, Lexington, Kentucky 40508–4008
www.kentuckypress.com

Unless otherwise noted, all photos and figures are provided by Karen Gorrell.

Cataloging-in-Publication data available from the Library of Congress

ISBN 978-1-9859-0306-7 (hardcover)
ISBN 978-1-9859-0308-1 (pdf)
ISBN 978-1-9859-0307-4 (epub)

Member of the Association
of University Presses

For Bryce, Larry, Les, Lois, Sam, Sonny, and others who will not see this book in print.

Those retirees were promised those benefits, and here in West Virginia, a promise made is a promise kept.

—WEST VIRGINIA SECRETARY OF STATE NATALIE TENNANT

Every retiree across this country deserves someone as passionate and fearless as Karen on their side.

—SENATOR JOHN D. ROCKEFELLER IV (D-WV)

They didn't count on somebody having the courage to stand up and raise hell and fight back.

—KAREN GORRELL

Contents

extension of women's positions as wives, mothers, and grandmothers. In their own time, activists like Eula Hall recognized health care as a human right. They dedicated their lives to improving health outcomes in communities bearing the brunt of contaminating and disabling occupations.

Karen Gorrell belongs to this tradition of Appalachian women, and thanks to Julia Flint, we can better know her and the people whose lives she changed. Like many activists before her, Gorrell drew on her position as a wife, mother, and grandmother to give shape to and sustain her work. Her activism was born out of her everyday life and the circumstances of caring and being cared for by her family. Through hard-nosed, grassroots activism, Gorrell built strong alliances across communities and helped others challenge Century Aluminum's broken promises. Out of these broken promises, Karen substituted her own: to see the fight through, to leave no one behind, and to carry the stories of those who spent their final months waiting on financial relief that never came. In doing so, she became a beacon of persistence and determination, demonstrating the power of individual actions within collective struggles. Through this work, Julia Flint also joins the tradition of illuminating what movements for change look like through the eyes of ordinary women whose life stories are otherwise difficult to track. Flint's ability to capture Gorrell's dedication and the resilience of the community she fought for adds an essential layer of understanding to the broader history of women's activism in Appalachia.

This collaboration reminds us that we tell our stories to lay claim to alternative possibilities that exist outside of what the system is prepared to give us or what it thinks we deserve. By sharing the experiences of Gorrell and the Ravenswood retirees, we further expose the injustices of a system that prioritizes profit over people, and we make visible struggles whose weight can only be felt on a human level. Their stories serve as a dramatic reminder of the human cost of corporate greed and the tireless efforts of individuals who refused to be silenced. Gorrell's voice, amplified by Flint's storytelling, now resonates with a chorus of others who have demanded more—more dignity, more care, and more justice. These voices are our tools of resistance that allow us to envision a future where caregiving is not only valued but integral to victories both large and small. They inspire us to continue to fight for a world where compassion and empathy triumph over exploitation and indifference.

Elizabeth Catte
Author of *What You Are Getting Wrong about Appalachia* and *Pure America: Eugenics and the Making of Modern Virginia*

Preface

I first met Karen Gorrell and the Ravenswood retirees in 2017. On a fall afternoon, I was traveling southbound on I-77 with my friend, Tom Breiding, headed toward Ripley, West Virginia. Tom, through his work at the Appalachian Institute (then at Wheeling Jesuit University), was hosting two groups of college students for weeklong service-learning trips, and I was joining as support staff. As we passed the exit for Ravenswood, the sign caught Tom's attention.

A few months earlier, Tom answered a call from an unknown number, and Karen Gorrell introduced herself. She had heard that Tom wrote and performed songs for the United Mine Workers of America. She was wondering if he might write a song for a group of aluminum plant retirees from Ravenswood, West Virginia, who had just ended a seven-year fight for health insurance benefits with a $23 million settlement. Tom shared some of the retirees' story with me, and I asked if he had considered inviting Karen to speak about her campaign to the student groups he was hosting. Rooted in the Jesuit education tradition, the service-learning trips combined volunteer projects with education on regional history as well as social and environmental justice issues. Many of these trips included presentations by local nonprofits or community organizers.

Despite the last-minute request, a minivan full of retirees arrived that evening to meet us. They were roughly the age of the grandparents of the students gathered as their audience. All but Karen and another woman had gray or white hair. The retirees sat in a row of blue plastic chairs with metal legs at the front of a fluorescent-lit, wood-paneled meeting room at one of the dormitory-style lodges at the Cedar Lakes Conference Center. Karen talked for well over an hour about the events in this book. She was confident, emotional, and inspiring. She said that she hoped others could hear this story, and afterward, I told her I wanted to help her share it. The retirees' story was compelling, and in the wake of the 2016 presidential election, the rest of the country seemed suddenly interested in stories from Appalachia. The retirees' settlement had recently been finalized, and I hoped to publish an article about their successful campaign.

Over the next year, I continued to meet with Karen and the retirees. I recorded and transcribed two of Karen's talks to students, attended one of the biweekly retiree meetings and luncheons, and sat with Karen at her home for a longer interview, where she handed over five large binders filled with newspaper articles, emails, photos, flyers, handbills, speeches, and other artifacts. She had scrapbooked the first five years of the campaign (and kept documents from the last two years in boxes, which she would share later). As I copied and cataloged these artifacts and outlined the major events that took place over several years, this book came into focus. I asked Karen and the retirees for suggestions as to what should be included and used their input to guide the first draft of the manuscript.

Seven years later, their story is being published. My goal is to honor Karen and the retirees' campaign and to document their contribution to West Virginia's long and rich history of labor activism. I also want to bring into focus the challenges faced by American retirees who have lost or are at risk of losing their insurance benefits. These reflect the challenges that all workers face as wages, benefits, and rights are chipped away and the wealth workers produce is funneled to the top of the pyramid—as executives and shareholders profit at workers' expense.

As this book evolved, I focused the narrative on Karen's life and attempted to include Karen's voice as much as possible. I tried to capture her personality, her talent and tenacity as an organizer, and the strength and determination that infuse her character. I also wanted to highlight some of the emotional highs and lows experienced in the decade that she and the retirees committed themselves to this cause (continuing even after the settlement was finalized). Because I did not grow up learning about labor history or hearing stories that honored or celebrated this region, it is important to me that the retirees' efforts are recognized. I also hope this book will inspire others to take a stand or speak up. I know that is also Karen's wish.

Amid the stories of addiction and despair, of poverty and the absence of opportunity that have largely defined national public perception of West Virginia (which, at the time I am writing, is my home), I hope Karen's story finds an interested audience. Her story reflects a different narrative of West Virginia and Appalachia—one of a people driven to stand up for what is right and to fight, when necessary, against the wrongs that have been done to them. Karen and the retirees are part of a legacy that stretches back for generations, of those who have voiced their truth and have said: Enough is enough. We will be seen. We will be heard. We will not back down until we have what we deserve. These stories, in Appalachia and elsewhere, should be shared and kept alive. It's important also to know that these efforts and those who lead them not only exist in the past but are lighting our path forward.

Author's Note

This is a story about West Virginia retirees who were faced with the sudden termination of their health insurance benefits beginning in 2010. The events and conversations in this book were recounted to me by these retirees—primarily, by the retirees' lead organizer and spokesperson, Karen Gorrell. It is Karen's story that I present to you, centering her recollection and interpretation of events. At times, I have added description, detail, or dialogue between retirees to re-create a scene, always with the intention to remain true to the story as it was shared with me.

Chapter One

Americans work hard each and every day under the promise that they will be treated fairly and with dignity. Sadly, far too many companies in West Virginia and elsewhere have abandoned the promise they've made to their workers through bankruptcy filings and other strategies to avoid paying their obligations.

—Senator John D. Rockefeller IV (D-WV)

Enough: August 2016

Karen Gorrell had barely slept when her alarm clock sounded. She was tired and nauseous, and she felt more acute anxiety than at any other moment she could remember in the last six years. She moved through her morning routine as if on autopilot, drying and styling her pixie-cut walnut brown hair. She applied eye shadow, a shade of blue lighter than her gray-blue eyes. She wore a pair of jeans and a casual dress shirt, with small gold earrings and a long gold necklace.

Eating was out of the question. She sat outside the hotel, waiting for the other members of the Century Aluminum Retiree Committee to finish breakfast. She then walked with them, saying little, to the United Steelworkers of America (USW) office building in downtown Pittsburgh, Pennsylvania. Inside the meeting room, she took her seat and looked around. Here she was at a table with the big dogs, as she called them—Century Aluminum's CEO, the vice president of the USW, and their lawyers. She knew she had given everything she had to earn a seat here, but still, she wondered if it was enough. Not if she was enough or if she had done enough, but she wondered how badly the odds were stacked against her and the retirees she was fighting for.

The purpose of the meeting was to begin negotiations for a settlement agreement that would fund health insurance benefits for more than 750 retirees and spouses of the now shuttered Century Aluminum plant in Ravenswood, West Virginia. Century had terminated contractually negotiated retiree health insurance plans at the Ravenswood plant beginning in 2010. Since then, Karen Gorrell and others had been protesting and organizing to pressure the company to reverse its decision. The USW, representing the Ravenswood plant's union workforce, had been fighting Century Aluminum in court on the retirees' behalf for just as long. In 2015, Century permanently closed the idled Ravenswood facility, and weeks later, a judge had ruled in Century's favor in the USW's lawsuit. Yet in 2016, the company's board of directors had agreed to discuss a settlement for the Ravenswood retirees.

The meeting room was uncomfortably warm, the air conditioner insufficient. Like the furniture and carpet, it, too, was likely a relic of earlier days. The USW had purchased the building in 1973, at a time when US manufacturing and the labor unions that represented workers still functioned like two pillars supporting an American middle class. The room felt like a time capsule. It was stuffy. Karen and her companions exchanged greetings with the others in the room. Then Mike Bless, CEO of Century Aluminum, addressed the group. "I wanted to acknowledge, before we get started, that if it wasn't for this woman's efforts," he said, gesturing to Karen, "we wouldn't be here today." Karen and the Retiree Committee had spent years fighting for a settlement, and that effort had led to this meeting, where they would represent the interests of retirees in the negotiations between Century and the USW. Bless shared Century's offer—the amount the company would agree to contribute to offset future costs for retiree health plans and related expenses. The total amount would be paid in installments over ten years into a voluntary employees' beneficiary association (VEBA) account managed by the USW.

Karen felt her heart sink as she listened to Bless. The Retiree Committee had argued for a onetime payment rather than a VEBA, believing it was the only way to fairly compensate retirees.

Karen knew the retirees had no leverage to get the deal they wanted most. What she hadn't known, walking into the meeting room, was that the mix of exhaustion, nerves, and nausea that she had felt that morning was her body telling her she had reached her limit. Before she could respond to Bless, tears started down her cheeks. It was automatic and uncontrollable, her body letting go of what she had kept herself from feeling leading into this meeting—the disappointment, the frustration, even the hope, all releasing as tears. She told herself she had given as much as a person could give, and in spite of every obstacle, she had believed that justice was possible. This belief, even when buried in doubt, was like an ember that she carried and could breathe life into when she needed to light a fire in herself or others. But she knew this was the end, and now she had to accept that the men and women she had fought tirelessly for would never get everything they deserved. They wouldn't get back what had been taken from them.

"It's not enough, Mike," she managed to say between sobs. "Hoot is already eighty," she said, pointing to Luther "Hoot" Gibson. "He's given up so much. We've all given up so much." She looked at the men with her, the other members of the Century Aluminum Retiree Committee. Each of them had worked at the Ravenswood plant decades longer than Century had owned it and had contributed a portion of their pay every hour to the retirement benefits that Century had ended abruptly.

"I wish all these men would live to be one hundred, and then maybe this would add up to something. But you know that's not going to happen."

Her tears didn't stop, and soon it became too difficult to speak. The men at the table sat in silence, as Karen did what she had not allowed herself to do since the evening she decided to fight Century Aluminum. She rested her head on her arms and wept.

If you asked Karen about her life leading up to this moment, she would say that it was ordinary. Before launching a campaign that would lead her to the negotiation table with an international labor union and a multinational corporation, she had considered her primary job being a full-time nana to her two (eventually, three) grandchildren. Born in 1950 in Parkersburg, West Virginia, Karen was the youngest of four children. She was naturally extroverted, confident, and always surrounded by a circle of friends. She married at twenty-one and worked jobs in retail and banking before and after raising her two children.

Faith and family are the most important aspects of Karen's life. She credits this to being raised by parents who both lived by a strong set of values. Her mother's were rooted in the church; her father's, the union. Bernice Irene Weaver Richards, Karen's mother, ran the Richards household, saw to it that the family attended church twice a week, and had little tolerance for bad behavior. She raised her children to do the right thing as a matter of principle. Once when Karen was in grade school, she and her sister accompanied their mom to the grocery store where the two girls returned the family's glass bottles and collected the deposit money. Karen's mom had also received a discount for the bottles when checking out, and when she realized the store had paid them twice, she packed Karen and her sister into the car and took them to return the money. It was only about one dollar, Karen remembered, but there was no question of doing otherwise. Karen didn't always value her mother's zero tolerance parenting style while living under her roof, but she came to appreciate how her own strong Christian faith was modeled on the example her mother set for her.

Harley Richards worked as a district organizer for the USW. Growing up, Karen cherished the occasional day when she went to work with her dad at the USW office in downtown Parkersburg. Endlessly curious, Karen asked questions about his work, and over time, Harley explained to Karen what a union offered workers and the values it stood for. Karen felt proud of her dad, sensing that his work was important. She sensed that it was dangerous too. Sometimes she overheard things that she wished she hadn't, stories that left her with a stomachache. Like how her parents once showed up at a union picket and were almost run off with baseball bats after being mistaken for company personnel. Or how there had been an explosive set off in someone's yard, blowing up a hole so big that a car could be buried in it. Sometimes, watching her mom sorting her dad's laundry after his work trips, Karen caught sight of a ripped, bloodstained shirt in the mix before her mom could hide it.

Later in life, Karen would say harshly that her dad was a proud union man from a time when union men didn't sit behind a desk and think that they could change the world with a pen. Her father's generation, and generations before, had been on the front lines fighting for the rights that many Americans would come to take for granted. US labor unions had fought to improve appalling working conditions, limit the workweek to forty hours, and set restrictions on child labor. They continued to negotiate for better pay, benefits, and workplace safety protections and to offer protection and benefits

Karen (age eighteen) and her dad, Harley Gorrell.

for injured or retired workers. Karen would admit that even she took labor's past successes for granted, however, not fully realizing just how valuable something like a quality health insurance plan was until it was gone.

Karen graduated from Parkersburg High School in 1967. She took a few classes at Mountain State Business College before meeting the man she would marry. At the time, Karen's closest girlfriends all had boyfriends and spent weekends together riding motorcycles to cookouts, back-road bars, and hangouts. Tired of feeling left out, Karen agreed to ride with a friend's brother, Mike Gorrell. Over time, she and Mike grew close. He was trustworthy, and Karen appreciated his directness and honesty. They married in 1971 and moved into a small cabin Karen's family owned before buying a garage apartment on land contract. At the time, Mike worked as a car mechanic making one hundred dollars a week, which was enough for them. But Karen's dad would help bring Mike on at the Kaiser Aluminum plant near Ravenswood, West Virginia, where the pay and benefits more than justified the thirty-mile commute.

Kaiser and the Ravenswood Aluminum Company: 1950–1991

While Karen was growing up, her home in the mid-Ohio valley—the region surrounding that long southbound stretch of the Ohio River that separates Ohio and West Virginia—was emerging as a prominent postwar industrial center. Just as West Virginia's coal mines had mechanized and reduced their workforce, the fate of these river towns would move in the opposite direction as men like Henry J. Kaiser, considered one of the nation's most influential businessmen, scouted locations for industry. Kaiser would build one of the world's first ore-to-product aluminum operations on an expanse of riverside farmland just south of Ravenswood, West Virginia, between the larger cities of Parkersburg and Huntington. The region was ideal for Kaiser's plant because of its location on the river, where raw alumina (aluminum oxide) could be transported by barge from as far south as Louisiana. The region also offered convenient access to coal, an economical and enticing source of power for Kaiser, who would sign the largest single power contract ever negotiated between two private firms for the Ravenswood facility.

Kaiser's Ravenswood plant began operations in mid-November 1957. By 1960, while the state's overall population had declined by more than 145,000 in the previous decade, the counties housing Ravenswood (Jackson) and nearby Parkersburg (Wood) were two of only a handful of counties in the state to see an increase in population. These expanding industrial communities—with their new homes and new schools and thriving downtowns—defied the War on Poverty images that would come to define the nation's perception of West Virginia. Within a generation, the rising tide of industry in the mid-Ohio valley had established a solid middle class of families, many of them raised on single incomes earned inside factories. (Like West Virginia's population as a whole, these families were predominantly white.)

As a district representative for the USW, Karen's father had been involved in organizing a new local USW chapter to represent the Kaiser plant's rapidly expanding workforce soon after the plant began operations. USW Local 5668 was chartered in 1958, and from the start, the union fought not only for pay and benefits but for health and safety protections as well. Like other manufacturing work, aluminum manufacturing had its dangers. Workers were exposed to harmful dust and carcinogens, volatile chemicals and gases, and extreme heat and noise. Many workers also did shift work, alternating between working days and nights, which was hard on the body over time. Still, the pay allowed workers to construct comfortable lives outside the plant. Taken together, the livable wage, strong union benefits, and promise of a secure retirement kept employees committed to Kaiser.

When Mike Gorrell started at the Kaiser plant in 1973, the relationship between management and the union was relatively strong, and jobs felt secure, even as the nation's manufacturing sector was showing signs of losing steam. By the early 1980s, a national recession and near saturation of the aluminum can market prompted layoffs throughout Kaiser's US facilities, including Ravenswood. Mike was just a few months into being laid off when he and Karen learned that Karen was unexpectedly pregnant. Their son, Chad, was still a toddler. It was terrible timing, but Mike picked up odd jobs to supplement the unemployment pay he received, and that kept the family afloat so that Karen could stay at home.

In 1989, the Ravenswood Aluminum Company (RAC) purchased Kaiser's Ravenswood aluminum smelting facility. The sale marked the beginning of a new era in Ravenswood—one that would put the union and the community to the test. By now, Mike Gorrell had been back to work for almost four years and counted himself lucky. He had just made the cut to return to work, while hundreds of others who had been hired after him were not as fortunate. The plant's workforce had been reduced significantly since Mike had been hired, and tensions between the union and management were escalating. Inside the plant's potroom, where raw alumina gets cooked at temperatures exceeding fifteen hundred degrees Fahrenheit, the ambient temperatures, especially in the summer, were hot enough to be dangerous, even lethal. Potroom workers were being asked to work double shifts, thanks to management's cost-cutting efforts, and they were collapsing from heatstroke, dehydration, and physical exhaustion. Four workers died on the job during the summer of 1990, and still, contract negotiations between management and the union had stalled by the fall. The union insisted on protections for workers' health and safety. The company, claiming that cost cuts were necessary to drive profits, refused to meet the union's demands.

On October 31, 1990, the day the existing contract between RAC and the union expired, RAC denied the union's request to extend negotiations. Management sent the union workforce home and locked the plant gates behind them, initiating a "lockout" that would last nearly two years. Mike Gorrell and around seventeen hundred other workers were out of jobs, and because RAC claimed the union workers voluntarily went on strike, they weren't eligible for unemployment benefits. The USW denied that claim. The case would be reviewed by the National Labor Relations Board (NLRB), and in the meantime, the USW provided funds that kept workers from the threat of bankruptcy. But bills went unpaid, and sacrifices were made. Karen had started working part-time at a bank after both her kids were in school. This helped curb the financial stress on their family, but Karen couldn't anticipate the emotional toll that these two years would take.

After locking the gates behind its workforce, RAC bused in "replacement workers" (or "scabs," if you were on the other side of the picket line) to fill the jobs the company's union employees were being prevented from doing. Historically, a strike or work stoppage was a means to put pressure on the company to negotiate with the union—no production meant no profits. By the late 1980s, however, industry's intensified use of replacement workers had undercut the union's primary bargaining tactic. As striking union workers walked out, companies like RAC were recruiting new workers, eager to earn a paycheck, to take their place. These scabs not only compromised the union's bargaining power but also threatened the sense of solidarity that could hold a community together during difficult times.

As a bank teller, Karen had to engage with the scabs directly. When that first RAC paycheck came through her line and she realized the position that she was in, she thought about quitting. Instead, she realized she could help the union by identifying the individuals working at the plant. Each time someone handed Karen a RAC paycheck to deposit, Karen would copy it and the person's ID and drop off a list of names at the union hall after work. While her employer might be "neutral," Karen was not, and she wasn't alone.

The picket line became a dividing line separating Ravenswood and neighboring communities into two camps: union and company. Union workers and allies avoided businesses sympathetic to the company. People stopped talking to family and friends. Some stopped going to church. Children were forbidden from going to friends' houses if their parents were on opposite sides of the picket line. Karen's own children stopped being invited into friends' houses. It was hard on everyone, but there was little room for one to waver. Union workers' livelihoods were on the line, and anyone who worked for or supported RAC threatened their chances of returning to work and the security and stability these jobs had provided their families. There was no safety net awaiting these workers if this job didn't pan out. The union job was the safety net. And now it was at risk. Because of this, scabs, in particular, were on the receiving end of the union's public harassment campaign. The union side wanted to send a clear message that the company's tactics and those who supported them weren't welcome in Ravenswood. Workers knew that their futures and their families depended on this ending in their favor, and they organized and fought as if their lives were on the line. Months passed by, then a year, and they had no idea when their fight would end.

Lockout: 1991–1992

"Hey, scab," Karen jeered in passing to a man she recognized from cashing his paycheck. She couldn't help feeling aggravated. She had to swallow her anger at work, and it built up until resentment was all she could feel when she thought about the people keeping the plant running, when it should have shut down and brought the company to the bargaining table. The man returned Karen's snide remarks with his own, and Karen stood her ground, raising her voice. She studied the man's clenched jaw and fists, aware of the other people around them. Their argument escalated, until, after telling him she had more pride in her little finger than he had in his whole body, Karen turned to leave. The man yelled slurs as she walked away, until Karen's son, Chad, then twelve years old, turned around and told him he better shut his mouth.

"You best listen to him," Karen told the man. She was surprised by Chad's outburst and was suddenly pained that he had to witness this. In the parking lot, seeing that the man was still behind them, Karen instructed Chad not to stop at their van. She was worried now. They walked a little farther down the row of vehicles and stopped in front of a small red sedan. She knew the man was trying to take down her license plate number, and if she didn't get into the vehicle, he would realize her bluff. She headed for the grocery store that stood in front of the mall, hoping he would lose interest. As a backup, she bought trash bags. Hoping she had stalled long enough, she rushed to her van to secure a folded bag over the license plate before driving home. She thought she was in the clear but soon saw the same man pull up behind her in her rearview mirror. She cursed the red light keeping her from turning onto the main street and cursed again when she saw a second man exit the passenger side of the car behind her and walk toward the back of her van. She jumped out of her seat before he could reach her license plate and told him to stop if he knew what was good for him. She instructed Chad, calmly, to walk into the Burger King and call 9-1-1. Then Karen waited, blocking traffic exiting the mall until the police came and gave her clearance to drive home.

Weeks later, Karen hurried out of the way of a car that sped by her as she was walking across a gas station parking lot. Weeks after that, Karen took Chad to a local park for a youth baseball game, where the man from the mall approached them. When he left and sped off in his truck, Karen's husband, Mike, followed him, wanting to make sure they had an agreement that this would be the last time he spoke to any of Mike's family. Karen hated the way she had felt during that time. She hated the tension in the air and hated worrying about what might happen to her or Mike or, God forbid, her kids.

Karen had put off seeing a doctor. Mike's company health insurance plan ended when the lockout began, and Karen knew they had to be careful with their spending. The bare-bones policy the union eventually offered was helpful, but Karen now considered medical care a luxury expense—one they would try to limit until Mike was back to work. Eventually, though, her heart palpitations got so bad she feared having a heart attack. There was no way she would risk leaving her two children without a mother, she told herself, deciding to finally visit the ER. After some initial questions and a brief exam, the doctor wheeled his stool next to Karen and asked politely if she was experiencing any extra stress. She sighed, embarrassed yet relieved, as the doctor looked at her with what she thought was sympathy.

"I've got the Emmett Boyle–itis, don't I?" she asked, laughing nervously. Boyle was the plant manager at RAC. "That man is causing all of us unnecessary stress."

It was around this time that Dottie Dalton handed Mike Gorrell an envelope and told him that she wanted him to take his family on vacation and get away from all this. Dottie owned a trucking company, and Mike did odd jobs for her to keep money coming in. No arguments, she told him. Those who were a step removed, like Dottie Dalton and Karen's doctor, could see clearly how after a year into the lockout, the stress was wearing people down. Karen couldn't see it herself until she was sitting by the pool at their hotel in South Carolina, watching her children play. She could relax here, and even the sky seemed brighter than it had a week before in West Virginia. On the drive home, Karen felt the tension return to her body. Her chest and stomach tightened as they entered Jackson County, passing the barns and highway overpasses spray-painted with the names of scabs—part of the union supporters' smear campaign. It didn't feel like coming home, she told Mike. It felt like returning to battle. Like their town was at war and their lives had been put on hold indefinitely.

What helped keep Karen going was what helped many people keep going—the community that came together in support of the union. She found solace and companionship in the company she met volunteering with the Women's Support Group, organized by Marge Flanigan and composed mostly of the wives of locked-out workers. In their homes and in the broader community, these women worked to maintain morale. They organized events, like a toy drive for Christmas, and prepared meals for gatherings. And when a court order limited the number of union workers permitted at the picket line, these women showed up in place of their husbands or male relatives. They also organized the daily "drive-bys," where the goal was to block traffic on the only road leading to the plant to prevent scabs from being able to get to work. Karen took part with dozens of other women on any given day, cruising at the pace of a barge drifting downriver, in a line longer than the town's Christmas Day parade, slowing the flow of traffic along the three-and-a-half-mile road leading to the plant.

Karen grew up in a union family, but the lockout gave her firsthand experience of what it meant to fight as a union, for the union. Throughout the experience, she felt the absence of her dad acutely. Harley Richards had passed in 1979. Karen knew he would have been fighting alongside her if he were alive. She felt she understood him more and what he had tried to teach her about union values. She was impressed by the unwavering commitment of the local and its supporters in Ravenswood and encouraged by the support that came from across the country—even internationally. Once, a bus of USW members from Michigan drove to Ravenswood to show their support and hand over a check in person. Members of that local, men and women who had maybe never stepped foot in West Virginia, had reached into their pockets to make a contribution to her community. The Women's Support Group had prepared a soup bean dinner for their arrival, and outside the hall, Karen could hear the bus horn blaring as it made its way off the interstate. Men and women walked off that bus smiling and cheering and hugged Karen like she was kin. She was told that other unions were standing with Ravenswood because they knew that if the USW lost this fight, it would cause a domino effect, and more locals would fall.

The USW is organized into local chapters (or "locals") representing one or more bargaining units. There are then twelve USW district offices, organized geographically, and all fall under the umbrella of the international office, located in Pittsburgh, Pennsylvania. While the Ravenswood lockout only involved one local, the USW International Office threw its resources into the fight, launching a national boycott campaign targeting beer and beverage companies who purchased Ravenswood aluminum for cans. As documented by Tom Juravich and Kate Bronfenbrenner in the book *Ravenswood,* in addition to the national boycott and the union's efforts in West Virginia, the USW followed the paper trail from RAC to the Clarendon Corporation and, by extension, to the commodities giant Glencore. Glencore was owned by Marc Rich, a billionaire on the FBI's most wanted list who had taken residence in Switzerland. Banking on the fact that Rich wanted to stay out of the spotlight, the USW focused its campaign on him directly, holding public protests at Rich's business headquarters in Switzerland and organizing rallies in countries where Rich's company was pursuing other business deals. It was a bold move, but if companies were going to new lengths to break the union, the union would also need a new playbook to survive.

The union's pressure on Rich eventually brought RAC to the bargaining table and gave the union a shot at getting Ravenswood workers back inside the plant. After tense and prolonged negotiations, the two sides reached an agreement on a new labor contract, ending the lockout. This was a fight that made labor history, which Karen learned in time. It was not common for a union to go to the lengths the USW had for a local strike with fewer than two thousand workers on the line. It was also expensive. But American labor needed a victory, and the USW—from staff at the international office to the Ravenswood union workforce—fought this battle as if every union worker in the country depended on it. Lockouts were becoming a more common strategy for companies to undermine workers, and the fact that the Ravenswood workers stood together made their fight stand out. At any moment, the locked-out workers could have turned their back on the union, joined the scabs, and returned to work, but almost no one did. In twenty months of being out of work, fewer than twenty workers out of seventeen hundred crossed the picket line.

For workers like Mike Gorrell who returned to their jobs in the plant after the lockout, the victory was bittersweet. The settlement was an outstanding accomplishment, but both sides had to make compromises. Juravich and Bronfenbrenner explained in *Ravenswood* that workers heard rumors that the NLRB would force RAC to compensate workers for the loss of pay during the nearly two years they were out of work. Instead, RAC claimed that if it paid workers what they were owed, it would break the company, and the USW agreed to drop the NLRB claim. It was a hard compromise, but workers had their jobs back. For those nearing retirement age, it was in their best interest to leave the past in the past, to keep showing up, and to pray that the gates stayed open. Retirement would bring a new appreciation for the challenges they would leave behind them. By sticking with the plant in Ravenswood through good times and bad, many union workers had made substantial contributions toward their retirement plans and pensions, and those benefits were worth what they had sacrificed.

Chapter Two

We are not rich in worldly goods, but we are rich in morals and determination. We are volunteers, veterans, preachers, Sunday school teachers, and nanas and papas, and we deserve better than to be tossed aside by Corporate America in their insatiable quest for profit.

—Karen Gorrell

Retirement: 1992–2010

After the lockout ended, Mike Gorrell was back to work in the potroom, but he hadn't been on the job a week when Karen got a call from the plant. Mike may have had a heart attack, she was told. She should come to the emergency room as soon as possible. When she arrived, Mike's body was surrounded by ice, an attempt to bring his body temperature below 100 degrees. He was soaked in sweat that left white stains on his clothes and skin, both marked with the scars of aluminum splash burns. Karen gasped. Over the years, Mike had come home from a number of double shifts, beyond exhausted, and tried to paint a picture for Karen of what it was like to work over an open cauldron, hot enough to melt metal. She couldn't comprehend it. Now, to see the full effects of that heat on the human body was chilling. No one knew Mike's prognosis, as some of the machines needed to run tests weren't functioning. Karen saw to it that he was transferred to a larger hospital and then thought of driving down to the plant to curse out management. She learned that Mike, and others, had been given ice packs to wear to keep cool during their shift—a practice implemented during the lockout. The problem, the doctor explained to Karen, was that the ice packs prevented the body from recognizing that it was overheating until it was too late.

Mike recovered, regained his strength, and returned to work, but it was no longer the work he loved. Morale among the union workforce never fully recovered after the lockout, in part because the plant kept some of the "replacement workers" on payroll. Mike's new work partner was one of these men, and Mike now had to choose between compromising his values or the job that he had just sacrificed for nearly two years to keep. He chose his job, begrudgingly, because the job was what was best for his family, and they would always be his highest priority. Mike continued to show up to work, without missing a shift, for another fourteen years before he became eligible for early retirement.

Mike was the primary wage earner and carried the family's benefits, so although he had been counting down the years, leaving the workforce was not a decision he made lightly. Karen was still in her fifties, and the couple needed to be sure they could afford to live on Mike's pension until they could each draw Social Security at age sixty-five. Knowing that health insurance costs would remain stable for their lifetime, thanks to the retirement plan negotiated by the union, was a significant factor in their decision making. It meant that even expensive chronic conditions could be managed financially. There wouldn't be any surprises.

"Not that you ever want to have to think about such things," Karen would say, "but we can't afford not to." The couple discussed their options at length with the benefits department at Century Aluminum, the company that now operated the Ravenswood plant. (Century Aluminum had taken over Glencore's aluminum assets, including the Ravenswood Aluminum Company [RAC], in 1995.) With every detail known and every dollar counted, Mike Gorrell retired in April 2006 after thirty-three years on the job. In retirement, he was able to spend more time with his family. Both of the Gorrells' children lived nearby, and the couple cherished the role they played in their grandchildren's lives. Mike and Karen became the primary babysitters for their two grandchildren, ages seven and six, and in 2007, they welcomed a third grandchild. The couple lived in the home they had bought shortly after Mike started working at Kaiser: a three-bedroom brick ranch house with a detached garage on a one-acre lot. They lived a good life and felt financially stable, even as the economy took a turn for the worse.

By 2009, the Gorrells were witnessing the effects of the Great Recession (the worst economic downturn in the US since the Great Depression) rippling through the mid-Ohio valley, though it felt like a low tide that had been receding for decades. West Virginia's population, along with the jobs that supported it, had been declining since Karen was born. The arrival of Kaiser Aluminum had acted as a safeguard for the economy in Ravenswood and the surrounding area, but the Ravenswood plant's workforce had also been declining since the 1970s. Now, the rest of the country just seemed to be catching up. Young people, even college graduates, struggled to find good-paying jobs, while layoffs seemed increasingly common among older workers. Large companies were shutting their doors, and it was no secret that Century was considering shutting down the Ravenswood plant.

In late 2008, the company had met with West Virginia state officials, including Governor Joe Manchin, to discuss the plant's fate. Century's management cited high operating costs and low aluminum prices as jeopardizing its ability to do business profitably in West Virginia. While the company was investing in building a new smelter in Iceland, spokespersons for Century said the company would need to cut costs at the

Ravenswood facility by $6 million a month, by February 15, 2009, for the plant to remain viable. On February 4, Century made its decision, announcing that it would idle the plant until further notice. Idling the plant meant that Century could restart operations in the future, but preparations were made to halt production, and within the month, 650 workers were laid off.

The news sent shock waves throughout the state. Although the workforce had declined over the past few decades, the Ravenswood plant remained an economic anchor for the region. Now the possibility of a permanent closure loomed. It was like living on a fault line, for a local economy to rely so heavily on one industry. The layoffs and downsizing of the previous decades were foreboding, and there was an underlying anxiety that one day the big one would hit: the plant would close for good. It wasn't just the number of remaining jobs lost that you had to consider, either, but the businesses those jobs supported—the shops and restaurants where people who earned enough spent their money—and the taxes paid by the plant and its employees. The ripple effects from the loss of a large employer like Century could transform a community. It had happened in the coal fields as mines were shut down. Those counties were now some of the poorest in the state.

On a personal level, Mike and Karen also worried about the possibility of Century filing bankruptcy and abandoning its retiree benefits. Specifically, they worried about health insurance. It was not altogether uncommon for companies to claim that retiree benefits were the ball and chain keeping them in the red. Bankruptcy might provide businesses legal measures to rid themselves of their responsibility to their former workforce. Other plants in the region had cut retiree health insurance, they knew. Fortunately, it didn't look like Century was headed toward bankruptcy, and as long as the company continued its operations (even if it wasn't operating in West Virginia), Karen and Mike understood that it was obligated to maintain the existing West Virginia retiree benefits.

It came as a shock then, in the fall of 2009, when Century mailed letters to retirees informing them that it would terminate the health insurance plans for many of its retirees aged sixty-five and older and restructure the plans for retirees under sixty-five. The new plan required retirees under sixty-five to pay a monthly premium and higher deductibles and copays. The sixty-five and older retirees, who had relied on Century's insurance as supplemental coverage for Medicare, would now have to purchase a supplemental plan or go without. While Medicare provides much-needed medical coverage for retired Americans, Original Medicare (Parts A and B) is not comprehensive, and unlike typical employer-sponsored health plans, there is no cap on out-of-pocket expenses that individuals are responsible for paying. Supplemental plans, like what Century had provided, help offset this cost-share burden and might pay for services not covered by Medicare, including dental, vision, and hearing. The company-provided health care was essential care for these retirees. Coming up with an extra $1,000–$2,000 a year to pay for supplemental insurance premiums could be a significant challenge for those living on fixed incomes.

The additional costs retirees under sixty-five had to take on were burdensome but not likely to bankrupt anyone. Unfortunately, after a year, in the fall of 2010, these retirees received a second letter from Century: their health insurance plans would also soon come to an end. Century would enroll these retirees in a COBRA (Consolidated Omnibus Budget Reconciliation Act) plan through June 2011. After that, retirees could elect to continue their COBRA coverage for another year if they paid the premiums. The difficulty was that COBRA premiums could cost as much as (and sometimes, much more than) the early retirees' monthly pension payments. That was true for Mike and Karen Gorrell, who would have paid more than $2,000 a month to remain insured with COBRA. Mike's monthly pension was $1,400. Unsettled by the news, both Karen and Mike decided they would need to start looking for work. Karen applied for several retail jobs that offered health insurance. It wouldn't be the same coverage Mike earned at the plant, but the premium wouldn't cost more than his pension each month either. Plus, Karen would earn a modest income to offset the additional costs. She knew that the pay in retail wasn't great, considering the benefits weren't all that great either, but they were decent jobs, especially if someone was fortunate enough to work full time. With her prior work experience, Karen had a good chance at landing something.

For Mike and others who worked as mechanics or maintenance crew in the plant, finding work at their age that matched their skill set and the pay they had earned at Century would be a lucky break. Of course, the ones who could look for work were fortunate. Some retirees were no longer able to meet the physical demands of a manufacturing job—or any job, in some cases. The men who had been hired in Kaiser's early years had worked with the fewest health and safety protections in place, as these protections were implemented over time. Some of these retirees now relied on oxygen tanks just to keep breathing. Others were homebound, bedridden, or needed walkers just to move from bed to bathroom to sofa and back. There were also younger retirees who were unable to work because of chronic illness. They would learn the hard way that without a job, health insurance was practically impossible to come by. Outside of employer-sponsored health-care plans, there were few to no options for these early retirees.

Eventually, the Patient Protection and Affordable Care Act (ACA) would open up options for early retirees to find coverage. Known by many as "Obamacare," the ACA was a national health-care reform signed into law by President Obama in March 2010 with a stated goal of making affordable health insurance available to more people. The law introduced new rights and protections for consumers. However, the law's components were rolled out gradually, and preexisting condition exclusions were not eliminated until 2014. Before this, someone managing a condition like diabetes, heart disease, or cancer could be denied coverage by an insurance company. Or these individuals could be charged higher rates, making coverage largely inaccessible.

The idling of the plant was hard to accept; however, the aluminum industry had been declining over time, and no one promised the plant would operate forever. Retirees were unwavering, however, in their belief that retirement benefits would last for their lifetime. They knew that without negotiating with the union, Century didn't have the legal right to make sweeping changes to the contract that stipulated what benefits workers and retirees received. These benefits were not handed out as an act of benevolence. Karen dug out the last "Master Welfare Benefits Plan" document Mike had, from 2007, which outlined the benefits provided by Century. It stated that Century had the right to amend or terminate the plan, "subject to union negotiations." Mike explained to Karen that Ravenswood workers regularly opted for lower take-home pay rates than workers in other plants because they chose to contribute more money toward retirement benefits. In 1984, for example, for every hour a union employee worked at the plant, they contributed around $0.92 toward the cost of retiree health care. By 2008, that amount had risen to almost $9.00 an hour. Workers viewed this contribution as an investment in their futures, like opening a retirement savings account. And they knew the toll their work had on their health meant that lifetime health insurance would be a necessity. The choice had seemed responsible at the time, but they took for granted that Kaiser, then RAC, then Century, would hold up its end of the bargain.

You Need to Fight: November 2010

In November 2010, a reporter called the local union hall in Ravenswood. Wanting to publish a story about the loss of health insurance for Century retirees, the reporter was hoping to speak with some under-sixty-five individuals affected by Century's most recent decision. The union sent notice to its members and scheduled a meeting that would give retirees a chance to come together. Karen and Mike Gorrell initially decided they weren't going to make the thirty-mile drive to attend. The reporter wanted to know what the retirees were planning to do, and that wasn't an easy question to answer. The Gorrells were upset and worried. They assumed buying health insurance, at their age, was out of the question. Karen hoped to hear back about a management position in retail, while Mike was still looking for a new job with benefits.

The morning of the meeting with the reporter, Karen started to think that maybe she and Mike should attend. She didn't have a good reason to change her mind. Nothing else had changed. But a thought entered her head and wouldn't leave. It didn't leave when she busied herself with cleaning the kitchen, then the bathroom, and next the living room or when she sat down in front of the TV to watch the news. Eventually, Karen told her husband that she thought they ought to go down and just hear what everyone had to say.

At the union hall, Mike introduced Karen to some of the men he had worked with. Karen met Bryce Turner, a tall, thin man with a face that would fit a preacher. His presence was peaceful and put one at ease, and Karen could have listened to him talk for hours. Bryce had worked most of his life as an ore loader at Century. He had worked at the plant for more than three decades by the time Century idled operations. Then, later that year, Bryce's health took a turn. A biopsy in December 2009 showed concerning numbers of blast cells (indicating leukemia), and Bryce was referred for an emergency consultation at the Cleveland Clinic on Christmas Eve. Without treatment, he was told, he would be dead in two weeks.

Bryce spent the next seven weeks at the clinic, with his wife, Cindy, at his side, undergoing treatment for acute myelogenous leukemia. His treatment included two rounds of dual types of continuous chemo, blood and platelet transfusions, and a barrage of testing and monitoring. The suddenness and severity of the illness shocked Bryce and made him realize that he needed to plan for what his family would do when he was no longer with them. His children were grown and independent, but his wife relied on his income and insurance benefits. Seeing no other option to keep them both insured, Bryce Turner submitted his application for retirement in February 2010. Once officially retired, he remained insured through Century. Though benefits had just been cut, Bryce and his wife were under sixty-five, so they would keep their insurance until they were Medicare eligible.

The doctors recommended Bryce receive a bone marrow transplant as soon as he was healthy enough to undergo surgery, but there wasn't a single match in the donor registry. Instead, he went home to West Virginia, where he was in and out of the hospital, first for a follow-up round of chemotherapy and then for hemorrhaging and a sudden drop in his platelet count. Then after two months of remission, Bryce was back at the Cleveland Clinic to begin a new type of chemotherapy. Throughout the spring and summer, Bryce continued cycles of chemotherapy approximately every six weeks, the timing depending on his blood test results.

Bryce's life looked nothing like it had two years earlier. From working full time in good health, Bryce was now laid off and fighting for his life against an aggressive cancer. If that weren't enough, in November 2010, Century mailed letters to Bryce and other retirees announcing that the company would end the health insurance plans for retirees under sixty-five. Soon afterward, Bryce was at the union hall with Karen and Mike Gorrell and dozens of plant retirees and their spouses, looking for answers. The workforce at the Ravenswood plant knew that their union contract guaranteed lifetime health insurance benefits, Karen heard again and again. There was no way the company could go back on this deal outside of a contract negotiation. Unfortunately, Century did just that and left it to the union and courts to prove that it was in the wrong.

That evening, Jodi Gorrell arrived at parents' house to find her mom lying on the couch, a pile of crumpled tissues on the coffee table. Karen shared what she had learned from Bryce Turner.

"Jodi, he's such a good person," Karen said to her daughter, still blowing her nose and wiping away tears. "He doesn't deserve what Century has done to him." She couldn't get over the fact that after everything he had accomplished in his life, after everything he had gone through in the last year, this was where he would end up—terminally ill and uninsured. Karen couldn't put it into words, but she felt the burden that Bryce was carrying as if it were pressing down on her chest and stopping her from taking in a full breath. She cried because she desperately wanted to help heave it away but couldn't.

"Mom," Jodi said eventually, sounding stern, but sincere. "Crying isn't going to change anything. You need to fight this." Karen was quiet. Jodi's response was not what she expected, and Jodi could see that. "I know you," Jodi went on, encouraging her. "You have more fire in your britches than anyone I've met. And I don't care if they're corporate America. It's not right. It's stealing. You can't just let them do this and get away with it."

Jodi, in her own life, had needed to summon this kind of courage and knew its potential. She also knew that Karen had it in her to take on this kind of fight. Jodi knew her mom to be uncompromising, even when challenged and even when it would have been easy and acceptable to compromise. From her perspective, her mom had never been a person to stay silent when she or someone she loved had been wronged.

Jodi thought about this, after she left her parent's home, remembering the time when, away at college, she got a call asking her if she had heard what her mom was up to. She could tell by the caller's tone that her mom wasn't in trouble but might be causing it. When she heard the details, she called a couple of sorority sisters and asked if they wanted to drive with her to Parkersburg, an hour and a half away. "My mom isn't going to do this alone," she told them. By the time they arrived, Karen had a small group of volunteers with her. They were gathered around Karen's van, parked on the road leading to the retail distribution center where Karen had been employed in the Human Resources Department. Weeks earlier, Karen had been asked to sign a disciplinary action form that had the effect of stating that she could not get along with others. She refused to sign it, denying the accusation, and put in her two weeks' notice instead. Afterward, she stewed over what had happened. When she heard from a friend at the company that the CEO and a number of investors would be visiting the facility, she decided she would make herself visible. She parked on the only road leading to the company's facility, the side of her van covered with handmade signs written on neon yellow poster board that laid out her grievances. "Favoritism in Wage Rates, Hiring Procedures, Benefits. Is that Company Policy?" one sign read. Karen stared down the out-of-state cars and held up her sign for who she presumed were investors and the CEO to read as they drove past.

Karen had a good relationship with some of the management team at the company's headquarters. She had a good relationship with several coworkers as well. She was a natural mediator and problem solver and cared about her employees. A supervisor had told Karen once that she cared too much and had even recommended counseling. That had been the beginning of the end of Karen's employment with the company, Karen thought, looking back. That evening after her protest, confident and indignant, Karen went to the front desk of the hotel where the CEO was staying and called to his room to ask for a meeting. He agreed to meet, and in the hotel lobby, Karen shared her account of the facility's workplace dynamics and politics and the circumstances surrounding her resignation. She wasn't asking for her job back, but she wanted to clear her name.

Years earlier, not long after the lockout, Karen had also quit her bank job in protest after an incident that resulted in two of her coworkers being fired. Karen thought the two women were being hung out to dry for something that, while technically against the bank's policy, was commonly accepted in practice. Karen was shocked and furious to hear that the women would not be able to collect unemployment because their termination was labeled as gross misconduct. She decided to go to their unemployment hearing to testify on their behalf, bringing evidence to support them. Then she quit. Karen told the bank manager that she didn't want to work for someone who would throw their employees under the bus to save themselves. They could stick this job where the sun don't shine, she said and left.

Civic Duty: November 2010–January 2011

Karen couldn't sleep the night after she met Bryce Turner. She tossed and turned, her mind always returning to Bryce, and to what her daughter had said. She had to do something. Karen also thought about the lockout, and about the commodities giant, Glencore, that still owned almost 40 percent of the stock in Century. The idea that a grandma from Parkersburg, West Virginia, could challenge corporate America was a fairy tale, if not a comedy. During the lockout, the entire chain of command of the United Steelworkers (USW), including the International Office, were involved in the union's campaign. Karen, as a retiree's spouse, wasn't even a union member. She had no authority. She had no experience organizing a labor campaign. But the longer she thought about it, the more she knew Jodi was right. The retirees couldn't sit back and expect their luck to change.

Early that next morning, Karen decided that she would plan a meeting like the one she had just returned from at the union hall. She wanted all of her elected officials present, reasoning there must be some action they could take on the retirees' behalf. She was convinced that if their representatives in Charleston and DC could shake the retirees' hands, look them in the eye, and hear firsthand the challenges they faced because of Century's actions, they would be moved as deeply as she was. If they could just hear Bryce Turner tell his story, they wouldn't turn their backs on him.

In an email to Senator Jay Rockefeller, Karen wrote, "I have spent much time over the years helping with elections, etc. and now we need your time." Karen considered that she had voted in every election since she was eighteen. She didn't think of herself as political, but she took her civic duty seriously. In her mind, she had held up her end of the bargain and had never asked for anything in return. She had never called her representatives. It had not even occurred to her until now. But at the very least, she thought, she would ask her representatives to look her in the eye and tell her that Century's actions were acceptable in the United States of America. She reasoned that if they weren't working to get Century to reverse its decision, they were complicit, and they needed to acknowledge that. The Ravenswood retirees, she would insist, needed their health care. They needed someone to hold Century accountable. They needed someone to give a damn.

Senator Rockefeller's office was familiar with the situation facing the retirees in Ravenswood, Karen learned. The senator had been involved in the unsuccessful effort to keep Century from idling the plant two years before. By the time Karen's letter arrived at his office, it was one of dozens asking for assistance for Century retirees. Wes Holden, deputy state director and director of constituent services for Senator Rockefeller, spoke with Karen when she followed up with a phone call. At the time, Holden was advising the Ravenswood retirees to connect with their union representatives. He wanted to facilitate communication, and believed it was in everyone's best interest for the union, with their clout and experience, to lead this effort. He encouraged Karen to have the union send the invitation to Senator Rockefeller and other elected officials.

"I can do that. I can contact the union," she told him. She paused and then added, "But I want to be honest with you. The retirees lost their health insurance, not the union. So, I don't care what the union does or doesn't do. We aren't going to stop calling or writing until we have our health care."

Karen scheduled her meeting to take place in mid-January 2011 at the USW local union hall outside of Ravenswood. She believed without a doubt that the retirees had a right to stand up for themselves in this fight, but she also knew that Wes had a point in asking the union to initiate communication. She had already written to Governor Earl Ray Tomblin (who had just taken over the office when Governor Manchin was elected to the US Senate) but decided she would take Wes's advice. On the retirees' behalf, the Local 5668 union president and the grievance chair cosigned a letter to the governor requesting his presence at Karen's meeting. Karen also asked the local union for a membership roster so that she could communicate with other retirees directly. Technically, the union couldn't hand out that list. But there had been thirty-nine retirees who had contacted the local about the loss of their health insurance, and it could give Karen those names and phone numbers. Karen called each one. Many were strangers. They knew Mike Gorrell, perhaps, but it was primarily this shared hardship that connected their lives to Karen.

On the day of her meeting, January 18, 2011, Karen arrived early. After doing everything she could think to do inside the union hall, she stood outside, smoking a cigarette, trying to calm her nerves. She felt anxious and a little out of place, but these feelings faded as retirees began arriving. She welcomed several faces that were familiar to her from the meeting she and Mike had attended in November. Having worried that the whole thing might flop, she thanked God that it looked like there would be a good turnout. By the time the meeting began, the hall was filled with retirees. Wes Holden from Senator Rockefeller's office was in attendance, as were representatives for Senator Manchin and Governor Tomblin. They heard the retirees' stories. They looked them in the eye and shook their hands. They promised that they would do what they could to help.

As Karen said her last goodbyes of the evening, she felt proud. She thought her dad would have been proud of her, too, and that meant the world to her. A few of the retirees in attendance said they had known him. Many more knew of him. Karen was following in his footsteps, someone had said. She hoped so. She felt the meeting had been a success, and this encouraged her. Bryce Turner and another retiree, Sam McKinney, had both addressed the crowd. Both of their stories made tangible the anxiety and anguish that the retirees felt.

Karen was grateful that the evening provided an opportunity for the retirees to come together. They were only a fraction of the hundreds of retirees who had lost their insurance, but that didn't matter. Many of the retirees were limited by poor health, Karen knew. Others accepted Century's decision as final. It was the way business worked these days. No one was going to throw a lifeline to the working class. The retirees who showed up did so because they were physically able and because it wasn't in their nature to walk away from what they were owed.

"Let us know if there's anything else we can do," these retirees told Karen as they were leaving, shaking her hand or hugging her. Out of the crowd that attended the meeting, there were more than a dozen retirees and their spouses whom Karen knew she could call on. These men and women, like Karen, had been writing letters and making phone calls. They were taking all the steps they could take, individually, and knew that their efforts would be more effective if they worked together. At home after the event, Karen pledged to herself that she would give her full commitment to the retirees' fight. She was ready and willing to organize the next step, though she didn't know what that step should be. So she prayed and asked the union for guidance, letting her contacts at the USW know they had a group of retirees ready and willing to take action. Karen emailed them regularly, either seeking advice or sharing information that she thought could help the cause. But she organized the retirees' campaign as an outsider. While the union was fighting Century in court, Karen began focusing her outreach on the state legislature, the public, other labor unions, and the upper management at Century. The lockout was not just fought in Ravenswood, she knew. In an email to her contacts with the USW, she referenced the lengths the union went to pressure RAC during the lockout and said she believed that this fight also deserved, and could gain, national attention. "We lit a little fire last week," she wrote, referencing her meeting, "but we want to create a bonfire." She added,

> We have to scream loud and long and make this a matter of national attention for all unions, all retirees, and all employees that will be facing this travesty if this is allowed to continue! I have taken the weight of this battle on my shoulders and I'm begging for your leadership. Please meet with us and give us direction and the full support of the union. We are fighters! You know we are! We will take this battle to Century once again! Let's force them to honor the contract or bring them to their knees once again! Let's make a difference together!

Karen took inspiration from the fact that these very same retirees, in the lockout, had already won one victory that few thought was possible. She saw no reason not to take this fight just as far if they had to. To that end, Karen explored all available avenues for support. "Contact the AFL-CIO," she was told by several people. "Or the United Mine Workers. They'll help you," she was promised. Karen tracked down every lead she was given but wasn't getting anywhere. People were busy. She was a grandmother, not even a union member, and she could tell she wasn't being taken seriously. By the time she made her fifth phone call to the AFL-CIO (American Federation of Labor and Congress of Industrial Organizations), Karen felt like she was hitting her head against a wall. Sherry Breeden, a political director and mobilizer with the AFL-CIO, had spoken with Karen more than once. She was sympathetic, and on this day, told Karen that she had called at a good time. There would be someone available to speak with her. As Karen waited, she could hear Sherry's muffled voice on the other end of the line, explaining that Karen had called several times.

"Listen," Karen said, interrupting Sherry's conversation. "Everyone told me to call your boss because he would be able to give us some advice. Everyone," she said. "But if he doesn't have the balls to call me back, he needs to be man enough to tell me, so I can quit wasting my damn time."

Sherry understood Karen's frustration. Having once spearheaded a campaign to push for employee pension increases at the racetrack and casino where she previously worked, she knew what kind of effort these actions took and how hard it was to gain ground. Whatever she could do and whatever connections she could offer Karen, she decided then that she would help. By the end of their conversation, both women had shed tears. Karen was comforted by Sherry's kindness and slightly embarrassed by her own outburst. That evening, however, she received an encouraging phone call from a retiree advocate who had been given Karen's information by Sherry, and that was progress.

Years later, Karen would be told by a friend and supporter working in the West Virginia Capitol that he had been advised, in these early months of her campaign, to think of Karen like a bee—a mildly disruptive presence that eventually, if ignored, would move on and become a nuisance for someone else. "Boy, was that wrong," he would tell her. What he would learn, and what Karen was learning herself, was that without credentials or a network of contacts, one of her most powerful weapons was persistence, and she had the will to wield it.

Chapter Three

Time is not on our side! We pray that you are!
—KAREN GORRELL

Choices: January 2011–February 2011

Jim Weltner was born in Parkersburg, West Virginia, and raised on a farm in nearby Mineral Wells until he joined the Marine Corps at eighteen. When he got out, in 1963, he heard that there were jobs available at the Kaiser plant. Good union jobs, with good benefits. "Ten weeks of vacation a year," some one told him. Jim didn't believe the vacation bit, but he still put in his application and hired on with Kaiser in March 1964. Jim worked thirty-eight years at the plant, and for the years that Kaiser owned it, he did get an "extended vacation" opportunity once every five years—three times in total.

Jim was retired seven years when Century first notified retirees that it was terminating health insurance plans. Like others, he turned to his state representatives to ask for help and attended the meeting Karen organized in January 2011. He called Karen afterward, offering his support, and explained what Karen was hearing repeatedly: health care was always understood to be a lifetime benefit. Jim knew this from having made the decision to retire initially in 1999. He had been warned that in the upcoming contract negotiations between the union and Century, which would determine workers' benefits package, the "Cadillac" health insurance plan workers currently had might be on the chopping block. Given how

T-shirt design by Karen's daughter, Jodi Damron.

much value Jim placed on having quality health insurance for himself—and especially for his wife, Pam—he retired early so that he could keep the "Cadillac plan" during his retirement. He then learned that the union had made other concessions during the contract negotiations and kept the existing insurance plans. Fortunately, because Jim had ultimately based his decision to retire on an assumption that proved false, he was given the opportunity to return to work. Then a few years later, when the same concern about having to downgrade their existing health insurance plans was raised again, Jim decided to retire for good. He wasn't going to test his luck twice.

* * *

At the retirees' third planning meeting, on February 14, 2011, Jim shared that he and Pam were devastated by the loss of their insurance plans. Jim was doing OK, being in relatively good health and having Medicare coverage, but he worried that Pam, who was not yet sixty-five years old, might not be able to continue with the routine medical care she relied on. Pam had suffered back-to-back heart attacks a couple of years earlier and quit working as a result. She relied on Century's insurance for routine health care and as a safety net in case of another health emergency. Jim voiced the concern that had been weighing on many of the men and women gathered around the folding tables at the union hall that evening: the tragedy of losing his health insurance was minimal compared to losing the ability to provide for his loved ones.

That night the retirees in attendance discussed a packet several of them received from the office of West Virginia congresswoman Shelley Moore Capito. Several retirees had written to or called Capito's office to plead their case and ask for assistance. As a result, Capito's office had contacted the Department of Labor's Employee Benefits Security Administration (EBSA) to request an investigation into the retirees' situation. After reviewing the documents provided by Century, EBSA determined Century had established its unilateral reservation of rights, which permitted the company to terminate retiree health insurance plans without the consent of the union. Representative Capito passed the message along to the retirees. It was a done deal, the letter implied. Case closed.

Karen remembered that someone at the United Steelworkers (USW) had explained to her that Century was going to argue they had a unilateral reservation of rights. "It isn't true," she was told, but she hadn't fully understood what that meant. What Karen did know was that while Congresswoman Capito might be satisfied with EBSA's ruling, Karen wasn't. That evening at the union hall, Karen worried about the effects of Capito's letter on the retirees' morale. It seemed to slash any hope they had been able to drum up to convince themselves that they could successfully fight Century. This was a clear case of corporate theft from workers, and Karen knew it, even if she didn't know how to prove it.

Sam McKinney was especially upset by the letter from Capito, Karen could see. Sam retired from the Ravenswood plant in 1996, the year Century took ownership, after working for thirty-two years. Sam and his wife, Ann, owned a bow hunting supply store, McKinney's Bow Hunting Den. They were both avid hunters and were active in several hunting clubs. Sam was a navy veteran. When Century canceled his health insurance, Sam was seventy-seven years old and had been retired fourteen years. In that time, he had a knee replacement, two strokes, open-heart surgery, and a total of six stents put in his heart. He used to tell his wife, Ann, that even though his pension wasn't much, he had good health insurance, and he thanked God for it. Now, Sam was afraid to think about what the loss of insurance would mean for Ann, who was just fifty years old, managing several chronic health conditions, and a long way from collecting Medicare.

The McKinneys had a combined income, including Sam's pension and Social Security, of $1,800 a month. They simply couldn't afford to take over COBRA (Consolidated Omnibus Budget Reconciliation Act) insurance payments for Ann when Century's payments ended in June. In fact, no insurance plan on the market would fit their budget. Even with Century currently paying for COBRA premiums the couple was still struggling. The price of Ann's medications had increased so much in the last year that she quit taking some of them. Sam had purchased a Medicare supplement plan for himself, but he was now paying three times what he had paid with Century's insurance for his prescriptions. Without asking his doctor, he had started cutting back on his heart medication to save some money. On top of the rising costs of food, gas, and utilities, these additional expenses for health care cut into the little extra money the couple had to live on.

Like Bryce Turner, Sam had shared his story at the meeting Karen had organized in January. He had said that he felt like his life didn't matter. In a written statement, Sam shared that "it seems as though, that after we have outlived our usefulness to industry, we are just supposed to give up and die." He lamented that "what was supposed to be my years of relaxation and enjoyment, after a lifetime of working, has turned out to be the most worrisome and stressful time of my life." He voiced these same frustrations at the retirees' February planning meeting. Sam had said he worried that if he or Ann faced a health crisis, the cost of treatment could bankrupt them. He could lose everything he had worked for. His voice was steady, but he paced himself in his speech, controlling his emotions. Though she had heard Sam's story before, it touched Karen just as profoundly as it had the first time.

"Sam, we're going to prove your life matters," she told him. The mood at the meeting was somber, and Karen felt a heaviness weighing on her as the group said their goodbyes and went their separate ways.

"You know, Ann," Sam told his wife on the way to dinner after the meeting, "the day I married you, I knew I could take care of you. Now, Century has stolen that from me." It was hard not to feel hopeless and upset thinking about their situation, but Sam tried to put his worries aside. It was Valentine's Day, after all.

In the parking lot of Outback Steakhouse after their meal, Sam reached out to open the door of their truck and paused. Ann, from the other side of the vehicle, asked what was wrong.

When Sam didn't respond she walked over to him. "Oh, honey," Sam said, when Ann got to his side, and then he fell to the pavement. A heart attack. A doctor who happened to be inside the restaurant pronounced Sam dead at the scene.

Karen heard the news the next day. She felt hollow. She had just met Sam. She had just seen him and talked with him and hugged him the night before. Valentine's Day. The shock stayed with her throughout the evening. It felt like the fog after surgery. There was a numbness that could only fade with time. The hollowness, though, began to fill. She was angry. Angrier than she had ever been, maybe. She was mad at Century but also at Capito for not questioning Century or EBSA and for sending the message that there was nothing to be done.

Karen knew that Sam had been cutting his heart medication pills in half to stretch each prescription over two months, since the cost had gone up. She knew, too, that at their age, prescriptions kept people alive. In 2010, more than two hundred deaths in West Virginia were attributed to someone not seeking treatment because of a lack of insurance. Nationwide that number exceeded twenty-six thousand. Sam's death was an individual tragedy, but it reflected a troubling statistic: thousands of Americans were dying from diseases and conditions that could be managed with proper and affordable health care. At the time of Sam's death, insurance companies could still deny coverage or increase rates because of preexisting conditions. Sam and thousands of others did the best they could with the options available.

Court Date: February 2011

Karen regularly emailed Century Aluminum's communications director Mike Dildine and occasionally the company's CEO

Logan Kruger but with no response. Eventually, frustrated with Century's silence, she would begin referring to Kruger publicly as Century's "chief execution officer." That was just the way she saw it. In February 2011, Karen wrote a letter to Kruger and Century's board, saying, "It is truly hard for me to comprehend how professional corporate executives could make decisions that create such devastation to the very people who have given so much of themselves to your industry over many decades." Referring to a recent press release in which the company announced that ending retiree insurance "increased current quarter results by $56.7 million with an associated discrete tax benefit of $2.0 million," Karen asked the men running the company, "Are corporate profits and multimillion-dollar compensations a reasonable exchange for human life?" She added that the retirees had been relatively quiet about the first round of benefits terminations, when the plans for the post-sixty-five retirees were ended. She guessed that Century's executives were "probably smiling all the way to the bank," and she made clear, "that phase is absolutely over." By now, Karen had been offered and turned down a management position in retail. She was fully committed to the fight for retiree health insurance.

On a weekday evening, less than a week after Sam McKinney's death, Karen received a phone call informing her that some higher-ups at Century were scheduled to appear at the Jackson County Courthouse the next day.

"I thought maybe you would want to give those Century bigwigs a retiree welcome when they get to West Virginia," the caller offered.

Karen hung up the phone and sat at her kitchen table, thinking over her options. Meeting Century was worth a shot, she decided, even if she only had a little over twelve hours to make something happen. If she could get a dozen retirees to show up, they would make themselves visible to Century's leadership, and who knew when they would have this opportunity again. Karen called Jim Weltner, Bryce Turner, and others she knew would be willing to show up, and asked them to invite anyone they could. Sam's death had shaken Karen badly, and she responded to her grief and her rage by vowing to take whatever steps she could. One death was one too many.

The next morning, Century retirees and their supporters filled the courtroom. After occupying every available seat, retirees leaned on the windowsills. Century's team would have looked out on the faces of dozens of men and women who called this community their home. Men and women who were eager to hear what their former employer, who had just terminated their health benefits, had to say. Eager, but respectful. The retirees didn't come with banners or large picket signs, and they weren't disruptive, except for the scare. From her seat near the front of the room, Karen heard gasps and commotion and felt panic start to rise through the crowd behind her after one of the retirees slumped to the floor.

"He only fainted. He's OK. Give him some space," Karen could hear, though she couldn't make out who it was on the ground. She did her best to stay calm, but her heart was racing. For a moment, she felt filled with dread, thinking that another retiree had just had a heart attack. The meeting was paused until an ambulance arrived, paramedics removing the retiree from the courthouse on a stretcher.

Century's visit to Jackson County related to its appeal of the county's appraisal of the Ravenswood plant's value, which determined the amount Century paid in property taxes. The company argued the value of their property should be lower. The cost difference mattered to Century, which claimed during the meeting to be pursuing all possible avenues to justify restarting the plant. One such avenue, Century's team noted, was a bill being considered by the West Virginia legislature that would provide the company a significant reduction in their annual electricity costs. This bill was considered a critical step toward resuming aluminum production. Century expected the bill to pass.

Karen couldn't believe it. She and a group of retirees met to discuss what they had learned and what they were going to do next.

"Century just admitted," Karen fumed, "that while they are trying to walk away from what they owe retirees, they are expecting tax breaks from the state worth tens of millions of dollars a year."

The retirees had been writing letters, making phone calls, and driving to Charleston to speak with their state representatives. These men and women knew the retirees were devastated by what Century had done. There was no way the legislature could be planning to pass this bill, the retirees reasoned. But Karen quickly discovered that Senate Bill 575 had indeed been introduced during the current legislative session. The bill, if passed, would convert millions of dollars in coal severance tax revenue into tax credits for coal companies selling coal to utility companies who sell power to "energy-intensive consumers" like Century. The coal company would be required to pass along the bulk of its savings from the tax credit to the utility company, which in turn, would pass on savings to those energy-intensive consumers in the form of reduced power rates. As convoluted as it appeared on paper, what it boiled down to for the retirees was that Century would be getting a substantial kickback for restarting the Ravenswood plant, without restarting retiree health insurance.

With the plant now idled for over a year, Karen believed Century was sending a clear signal that it was willing to walk away from West Virginia if things didn't go its way. She assumed

Karen addresses a crowd at the Century Retirees Rally in Charleston, West Virginia.

Century's management was counting on the company's influence as a major employer in the state, and she now had a better understanding of the impact Century's closure would have. Appalachian Power Company, which provided Century with electricity; the coal companies, which sold coal to Appalachian Power; the USW, which represented Century's workforce in Ravenswood; Jackson County, which collected taxes from the plant—they all had an interest in seeing the Century plant producing aluminum. Taken together, the loss of jobs, the loss of tax revenue, and the loss of a major utility contract would be a disaster.

The retirees also wanted the plant to reopen, but they had to take a stand: until Century paid its debt to retirees, the state shouldn't hand Century a dime. If no one else were willing to say this, they would.

"We're going to Charleston," Karen told the retirees, "and we're going to kill that bill."

A Moral Issue: February 2011–March 2011

For most of the year when the state legislature is not in regular session, the West Virginia Capitol complex has a quiet museum-like atmosphere. The garden beds are meticulously maintained—tulips and dogwoods filling the grounds with bursts of color each spring. The sidewalks are seldom crowded. At the north end of the complex, a two-story limestone and granite memorial honors the more than ten thousand West Virginians who died in the wars of the twentieth century. To the south, the front steps of the Capitol descend toward the Kanawha River, where millions of tons of coal have been transported by barge to the Ohio River, beginning before railroad and overland routes were established. The Capitol building, built between 1924 and 1932, is crowned by a gold-plated dome that dominates the skyline.

The decisions made inside the Capitol building impact the lives of every West Virginia citizen, but most of the time, that's easy to forget. In sixty years, Karen never found a reason to step inside the marbled halls or stand beneath that gilded dome, and this was true for many of the Ravenswood retirees. But now that Karen knew the "Century Bill" was scheduled for a vote, she made it her mission to stop it. She and the retirees planned a letter and phone campaign targeting the bill's sponsors while continuing to raise awareness of their situation among the broader legislature. Their efforts culminated in a rally at the Capitol during the first week of March 2011. The retirees had already made several trips to the Capitol and walked through every open door, passing out handbills and sharing their story. The governor's door had remained closed so far, but Karen was encouraged when the Democrats overall were sympathetic to the retirees' situation. Republicans in general seemed less concerned. If Century needed to cut costs to reopen, that was their business, the thinking went. Karen didn't let this deter her, insisting that what happened to the retirees was not a political issue, but a moral one.

Bryce Turner wrote to the Century bill's sponsor, Senator McCabe, arguing that while Century claimed it needed to cut costs (retiree insurance) to restart the potlines in Ravenswood, it was also paying to build a new potline in Iceland. Before Century could consider offloading more costs onto West Virginia taxpayers, he said, the company needed to fulfill its existing contract obligations. He included a document that detailed his battle with leukemia, explaining that he had been recruited by the wife of a retiree to share his story. "If you have not come across the name Karen Gorrell yet through all of this, I am sure you will," he wrote to the senator. In Karen's email to Senator McCabe, she reprimanded the state for negotiating with thieves, saying, "Jobs are very important to this state but not on the backs of the retirees! They may rob our health care, but our state does not have to be held hostage by this outlaw corporation." In what would become a signature phrase, Karen called Century's termination of the retirees' health benefits "murder without a gun."

The retirees knew that the region wouldn't be the same if the Century plant didn't start producing aluminum again. They wanted a stable future for their children and grandchildren, and they believed that future depended on jobs at the Ravenswood plant. Some retirees working with Karen even volunteered to help restart the plant and to train a new workforce. They were clear that they did not want to stop the plant from operating, but they did want to see the retirees given what they were owed after they had kept the plant running night and day for decades. If that meant postponing the restart, that was Century's problem, as far as the retirees were concerned.

The company had jeopardized far more than the plant's future when it turned its back on its retirees.

Fortunately, although they didn't know it at the time, the retirees had support inside the Capitol building. On March 2, 2011, two days before the retirees' scheduled rally, the West Virginia Senate Finance Committee met and voted down the Century bill, preventing it from moving forward for a vote in the Senate.

Karen was leading a TOPS (Taking Off Pounds Sensibly) meeting when she received a text saying that the Century bill had stalled in the Senate Finance Committee. She didn't hold back her excitement, exclaiming to the women in the room, "We killed the bill!" The next morning at 6:00 a.m., still buzzing with adrenaline, Karen sent an excited email to supporters after seeing confirmation on the morning news. "We are still having our rally!" she wrote. "It's still important to stay out there! Our message is beginning to extend beyond the West Virginia borders and it's important to keep it going!"

The following day, two charter buses arrived in Charleston with dozens of retirees and their family members. It was the retirees' biggest and boldest gathering to date, and following news that the Century bill had been stalled, it garnered attention. News reporters, journalists, and photographers greeted the retirees. Photos of the event showed gray-haired men and women wearing blue jeans and bright blue shirts. The shirts were designed by Karen's daughter, Jodi. They included the text "Century Aluminum Robbing Retirees of Life-Sustaining Contractually Promised Healthcare!" Below this were two bright red handprints with the words "Our Blood Is on Their Hands" written across them. The back of the shirts, in a nod to the lockout, had "One Day Longer, Again" printed in large bold letters.

The retirees had organized this event as a rally, not a celebration, but it was a monumental moment. The legislature was on their side. They had killed the bill. Of course, not everyone in the legislature agreed with the Finance Committee's decision. Representative Karen Facemyer was quoted in multiple papers expressing her disappointment. She was livid, one paper said, and while she was aware that former Century workers were coming to the Capitol, she seemed unclear about their mission. She reprimanded her colleagues who had stopped the bill, saying she didn't know how they could sleep at night, having pulled the plug on the plant restart. She challenged them to look Century's retirees in the eye and explain their decision. During the rally, Facemyer was booed by retirees when she walked toward Karen and the others gathered to address the crowd.

Karen stepped forward to speak to Facemyer, introducing the senator to Bryce Turner. Karen spoke of Bryce's tenure in the plant, his family, his role in the community, and his cancer diagnosis. "If you can look this man in the eye," Karen said, "and tell him that opening the plant is more important than his life; then go ahead, try to get that plant started. But that's on your conscience."

Karen's unapologetic accusations and demands would become characteristic of her public speeches and interviews. Already, reporters were taking notice, putting her words in circulation throughout the state. "Logan Kruger and Century Aluminum can kiss our hind end," the *Charleston Gazette-Mail* wrote in their coverage of the rally, quoting Karen, who had stepped into the role of retiree spokesperson. It suited her. She had never had a problem looking someone in the eye and saying what needed to be said, and she didn't say anything to the press that she wouldn't say directly to someone's face. She also understood the necessity of keeping the retirees' story in the public eye. She knew Century, and others, assumed it would only be a matter of time before the retirees grew tired of holding signs and writing letters. Sooner or later, they would accept the company's decision as a burden they had to bear. But not yet. Not today. Today the retirees were standing between Century and a deal worth millions to the company.

It's Not Us: March 2011

In its coverage of the rally, the *Charleston Gazette-Mail* reported that the USW wasn't taking a stand against the Century bill, though the USW wanted Century to consider reinstating retiree insurance. Karen had spoken with a USW representative during the rally who shared that someone from Century had approached him inside the Capitol, wanting to know what the hell was going on outside. The union representative had to tell him, "It's not us. The retirees are coming after you themselves."

It was true that Karen led the retirees' charge independently of the union, but she kept her contacts at the USW up to speed on her plans and sought them out for advice or support. After the Charleston rally, Karen would acknowledge Randy Moore, subdistrict director for the USW, for helping the retirees engage with their elected officials and amplify their outreach. At the local office, grievance chair Eli Morris attended retiree-planned events and wrote letters on their behalf, encouraging the retirees' efforts. Responding to Karen's request for guidance, he had urged Karen to keep her fight in the public eye and to continue engagement with both the state and federal governments.

As promising as it was to know the Century bill wouldn't become law, the West Virginia legislature wasn't forcing Century to reinstate retiree insurance, and there was still the possibility that Century would permanently close the Ravenswood plant. Karen intended to build on the energy and optimism generated by this win, but she knew it wasn't enough to focus on Century's bottom line. In her mind, the most important issue wasn't the money. This was about the lives of retirees and the drastic impacts of Century's decision on individuals and families. These were real people, not "liabilities" on a balance sheet, and if the retirees were going to get their insurance back, Karen knew they would have to get that message across to Century.

To that end, Karen was organizing a trip to Cleveland, Ohio, the home of Century's board chair, and to Hawesville, Kentucky, the site of another Century Aluminum plant. If they could raise some money, Karen also wanted to make the trip to Century's headquarters in California. Each event would help spread the retirees' message to a new audience. At the same time, travel was costly and a big undertaking for the retirees, given their age. What Karen really wanted was national media coverage. She had already reached out to *Mother Jones* magazine, film producer Michael Moore, and *The Ed Show*, a weekly news talk show hosted by Ed Schultz on MSNBC. No one had responded. But Karen remained convinced that she just needed to reach the right person. Hopeful and inspired by the stalling of the Century bill, she wrote to the president of the USW, Leo Gerard, introducing herself and asking if Gerard could support the retirees in securing an appearance on *The Ed Show*, where he had been a guest previously.

Gerard responded that Karen's introduction was unnecessary, as she was well known throughout the union and her work on behalf of retirees had brought important attention to the retirees' concerns. He wasn't optimistic about the retirees securing time on national television, however. Gerard cautioned her that national attention on the retirees' situation could be a double-edged sword, in that it could inspire other employers to follow Century's example. The better course of action would be for the union to win the retirees' case in court and set a legal precedent for the protection of retiree benefits.

As an international labor union, the USW's priorities and responsibilities stretched far beyond the retirees in Ravenswood. Intensive campaigns challenging each company that tried to skirt its obligations to retirees weren't a feasible route for the USW to take. Still, in his email, Gerard praised Karen's efforts and expressed the union's commitment to continuing to fight on behalf of workers and retirees. He also encouraged Ravenswood retirees to get involved with the Steelworkers Organization for Active Retirees, or SOAR, created in 1985 as an affiliate organization for retired USW workers. The stronger the SOAR membership, the more effective the organization could be in advocating for retirees' interests.

Karen was disheartened. People she loved were suffering, and she was willing to go to whatever lengths were necessary to fight Century. She knew others willing to go with her. Working within the traditional avenues available to them, the court case or advocacy through SOAR, wasn't enough. SOAR actively supported Karen's efforts, sponsoring the retirees' rally in Charleston, but several retirees were offended that retirees were grouped in a separate organization. Until this fight, the retirees organizing with Karen had not acknowledged any distinction between active and retired USW membership. When the distinction was introduced at a meeting with the union, the retirees' takeaway was that, technically speaking, retirees were no longer USW members. This didn't sit right with some. After being cast aside by Century, it again felt like they were being told their decades of union dues and sacrifices didn't matter.

Still, the USW did fight for the Ravenswood retirees: supporting their organizing efforts, providing them with a meeting location, and representing the retirees' case in court. By the time the first benefits termination letters from Century arrived in November 2009, the USW was filing its case against Century in an Ohio court. Though the plant and the majority of the workforce were located in West Virginia, there were a significant number of retirees living just across the Ohio River, and there was the perception that Ohio, compared to West Virginia, offered a more level playing field for labor. The union's case would not be judged in Ohio, however. Anticipating a legal challenge from the USW, Century had already filed a case in a West Virginia court, asking the judge to verify its right to terminate the retirees' health plans.

The USW's case was transferred to West Virginia and merged with Century's preemptive case. The judge then dismissed the USW's motion for a preliminary injunction, which would have required Century to continue to provide retiree health benefits while the case was being decided. That alone would have allowed the retirees to breathe a sigh of relief. It could have saved Sam McKinney's life, Karen believed. But because the USW did not seem likely to win this case, the judge would not require Century to continue to provide retiree insurance benefits while it slogged through the courts. The USW would appeal this decision; however, by the time of the retirees' rally in Charleston, a ruling on the appeal was still months away, and nothing about the court case was inspiring confidence. Karen was disappointed to have to accept that the outcome of the case could depend on the location of the trial. Or the politics of the judge. Or who knew what else. It seemed arbitrary and unreliable. In the last few months, Karen felt that for the first time in her life, she was pulling back the curtain and taking a closer look at the workings of

America's legal, political, and economic systems, and it all appeared less dependable than she had once imagined. She had believed that a signed contract was as good as a man's word, for example, and that the court system would protect the average American against wrongdoing. But neither seemed to be true now.

Chapter Four

We need to fight this war like it was meant to be fought, not in a broken court system, not at a desk, but in the streets and in the media and across the country.

—Karen Gorrell

Chagrin: April 2011

By late morning on April 4, 2011, it was already a miserable day in Cleveland, Ohio. The rain was relentless, the wind biting, and the sky dense with gray clouds. Still, Karen was hopeful. She and a caravan of retirees and their spouses had just arrived at the Saint Luke's Foundation office, located between Shaker Heights and Central Cleveland. They parked their rented minivans, gathered their handbills and picket signs, and filed through the building's front doors.

"We are retirees of Century Aluminum in West Virginia," Karen explained to the receptionist, who looked suspiciously at the group. "We're here to bring attention to the actions of one of Saint Luke's board members, John O'Brien," she continued, handing the receptionist the information packet she had prepared. Karen's tone made clear that she was not asking permission.

The Saint Luke's Foundation is an organization dedicated to improving individuals' and families' health and well-being in the Greater Cleveland area, according to the foundation's website. From the retirees' perspective, the commitment to improving health and well-being didn't square with O'Brien's decision (via Century's board) to terminate hundreds of

Retirees protesting in Cleveland, Ohio.

families' health benefits in West Virginia. They wanted him and all of Saint Luke's to give this discrepancy some consideration.

As chair of the board of Century Aluminum, John O'Brien earned $281,000 in compensation in 2009. By comparison, Karen wrote in the handbill for this trip, most retirees' total household incomes were less than $3,000 a month, or $36,000 annually. Karen didn't doubt O'Brien was a good person, and she wanted him to recognize the true cost of terminating health insurance benefits for elderly, working-class Americans. Karen told the retirees they needed to find one board member, just one, who had a heart. O'Brien was an obvious starting point, not only as the chair of the board, but also as the only board member residing within a half-day drive from Ravenswood.

Outside Saint Luke's, the retirees began their picket and were promptly asked to leave the premises. Expecting such a reaction, they obliged, moving beyond the building's fenced perimeter to the sidewalk. For over an hour they tried to keep their heads high as the wind brought rain down in sheets, turning their umbrellas inside out, soaking their signs and handbills. Karen's optimism faded. At sixty-one years old, she was the youngest of the group. The oldest was seventy-five. Taking a step back, she looked at her companions, now drenched from the cold rain. She had just watched Larry Williams, cane in hand, limp across a busy street to chase his picket sign, after the wind ripped it from his wet hands. She considered that if someone in the group caught pneumonia, it could be the end. Yet here they were, risking their health because their employer had wrongly terminated their health insurance. The whole country ought to see this and know what Century is doing, Karen thought. At the very least, John O'Brien ought to see this.

Karen knew that word of their appearance would reach O'Brien, but after driving all morning and picketing in the rain, she wasn't giving up on meeting in person. The retirees had an address for Inglewood Associates, a consulting business owned by O'Brien in the nearby town of Chagrin Falls, and they decided they should cover as much ground as possible. Ron "Ripcord" Dixon and his wife, Betty Jane, led the caravan from downtown Cleveland to the address for Inglewood. Instead of an office building, however, they found themselves in a residential neighborhood in front of an impressive white home with a For Sale sign in the yard. The address must be wrong, Karen thought. She questioned a neighbor who happened to be outside and, to her surprise, confirmed they were at O'Brien's office. His home office. The family was vacationing in Florida.

Out of pure curiosity, and a touch of prodding on the part of her companions, Karen called the number for the realtor listed on the For Sale sign. It was a gorgeous house, and she wondered what it was selling for. Certainly more than the homes in Jackson County, she thought. While her companions snickered like school kids during a prank phone call, Karen tried to keep a straight face as she declined the realtor's offer to tour the home. "No, that's okay, I was just curious," she said. She had other business to attend to. The group again filed out of their minivans with picket signs and handbills, and it didn't take long for the residents of Water Street to take notice. Karen took it on herself to call the town's paper and announce the picket, while a neighbor took it on themself to call the police.

Sirens wailed as red and blue lights flashed into the homes of O'Brien's neighbors. The retirees watched the two cop cars approach without putting down their signs. They had no qualms about talking to the police. In fact, they welcomed the opportunity to thank the officers for collectively taking a stance against Ohio's Senate Bill 5, which restricted Ohio public employees' ability to strike or to bargain for health insurance or pensions. Unions across the country had their eyes on Ohio.

The retirees' clothes were still soaked from the morning rain as they explained their mission to the responding officers, who left without issuing any citations. Shortly after, Karen watched a car approaching slowly down Water Street, stopping near O'Brien's home. A well-dressed woman wearing heels and a worried expression approached the picket. "The realtor," Karen said under her breath.

"Is Karen here?" the woman questioned, glancing from the retirees' faces to their picket signs. A few of the retirees exchanged their own nervous glances. Karen stepped forward to talk to her.

"No, ma'am. She went home about thirty minutes ago," Karen responded before anyone could give her away. It was just a white lie, she told herself, feeling a little guilty but mostly relieved as the woman returned to her car and drove out of sight.

On their way out of town, the retirees left handbills at each office in city hall and with every business on the main street in downtown Chagrin Falls. As they hit the highway, they had a good laugh about the whole thing and told themselves that if O'Brien hadn't heard about their visit already, he would soon. The entire town would hear about it, in fact, because the retirees' story made the front page of the *Chagrin Valley Times*. In the accompanying photo, ten retirees line the sidewalk in front of O'Brien's home holding handmade signs reading "John P. O'Brien should support the health and wellbeing of Century Aluminum Retirees" and "Retiree blood is on Century's hands."

Following the trip to Cleveland, Karen sent out a long email to her campaign email list, sharing the highlights of the trip, including praise for the drivers, Ron and Betty Dixon: "We only missed one exit!" She ended by saying that everyone involved agreed they had accomplished much more than they expected. From not knowing where or how to start, the retirees were now building momentum. Karen was leading the charge, and her sense of personal responsibility for the retirees' fight increased as time passed. She was becoming consumed by the work. "I was obsessed," she would say years later, reflecting on this time of her life. "There was no other word for it."

Karen heard new stories from retirees each week, it seemed, and each one felt like adding salt to a wound that wouldn't heal.

Wes Holden, Mike and Karen Gorrell, and Senator Jay Rockefeller at the Gorrells' home in 2012.

There was Gus, who had survived a heart attack and open-heart surgery before Century cut off his insurance. The prescribed medications for his heart condition cost nearly $1,000 a month. Like Sam McKinney, Gus opted to stop taking the medicines so he could continue paying other bills.

Dorsey retired from Century early for health reasons and had been out of the workforce for more than a decade when Century terminated his health insurance. He'd had three heart attacks and was struggling to afford the prescriptions required to prevent another.

Then there was Bill, an early retiree with diabetes. When Century terminated his policy, he made calls to fifteen different insurance companies. Each one denied him because of his preexisting condition. He even contacted the West Virginia insurance commissioner who told him there likely wasn't a policy in the state that would cover him, given the circumstances. Paying for COBRA (Consolidated Omnibus Budget Reconciliation Act) coverage was out of the question on his limited income, which left him with only one option: go without insurance until he was eligible for Medicare.

Adrian, who had worked at the plant for nearly thirty-nine years, had a blood condition that required regular bloodletting treatments. His condition worsened at the same time Century announced it would end his insurance plan. Even with Medicare, he was paying nearly $12,000 out of pocket annually on health expenses, including more than $2,000 for insurance premiums to replace the supplemental plan Century had previously provided.

Early Retiree Reinsurance Program: April 2011–May 2011

Karen looked at the time on her computer—almost 9:00 p.m. She rubbed her eyes, rolled her head from side to side to ease the tension at her shoulders, and walked to the porch to smoke a cigarette. She had been at her computer for hours. She was tired. Her eyes ached. She realized, passing the dishes in the kitchen sink, that she had not spoken more than a few sentences to her husband in the last twenty-four hours. She had barely left her office.

The day before, April 19, 2011, a letter had arrived from Century Aluminum. It notified the retirees that they already were "a plan participant or [were] being offered the opportunity to enroll as a plan participant, in an employment-based health plan that is certified for participation in the Early Retiree Reinsurance Program (ERRP)." Bryce Turner was the first to call. He had read and reread the letter before Karen had been to the mailbox.

"This could be a miracle for us, Karen," Bryce said, explaining what he had read about the insurance plan. Karen wasn't so optimistic and hated to have to tell him so. Of all people, she didn't want Bryce to lose hope.

"Bryce, I wish to God I could trust them to do the right thing, but I don't think we should get our hopes up until we know the details. Let me check the mail and I'll call you back."

Damn them, she thought as she hung up the phone. *What are they up to now?*

According to the letter in Karen's hands, Century Aluminum had accepted funds from the ERRP, a program created through the Affordable Care Act to provide financial relief to employers and employees facing the rising costs of early retiree health plans. Some employers had already taken the matter into their own hands, terminating retiree plans, a trend that had been developing over decades. In 1988, 66 percent of large firms in the US that provided health insurance to their active workforce also offered retiree health insurance benefits. By 2010, that number had dropped to only 28 percent. The ERRP's website acknowledged that without employer-sponsored insurance, many early retirees could not afford health insurance costs without significantly impacting their life savings. The $5 billion in funding that the program offered to US companies was an effort to keep these early retirees insured at rates that were affordable.

Karen was familiar with the ERRP. In an article published in November 2010, Erica Peterson wrote for WV Public Broadcasting that Century had applied and been accepted into the program, but the company planned to terminate retiree insurance plans regardless. The company noted that it regretted the decision. Tom Conway, international vice president of the United Steelworkers (USW), said his understanding was that Century simply decided not to bother with the ERRP money, even though it could extend insurance plans for its retirees. Karen had not given the ERRP a lot of thought recently. But months had passed with no news of this program, and she had to wonder, why now? Karen prayed that the letters were backed by good intentions. She knew Century's track record, though, and didn't want to give the company the benefit of the doubt.

Karen read the letter a second time and then called Century's Benefits Department in Hawesville, Kentucky, which was now handling the West Virginia benefits plans. When Karen got someone on the line, she was told that Century was choosing to use the funds to reimburse the money they had already contributed to pay for retiree COBRA plans. It would not use the funds to pay for any additional coverage. Karen gripped the phone to her chest as she slowly exhaled, telling herself to keep her cool.

"Well, I expected as much," she said and considered hanging up before saying something she would regret. She continued anyway. "I don't know how anyone could work for a company this despicable. How could you put a stamp on the envelope to this letter knowing what these retirees are going through?" Then she hung up, fuming. She paced next to the dining room table, phone in hand. This had to be illegal—there was no way Century could pocket money that was supposed to offer a lifeline to retirees.

She called Bryce to tell him, "It doesn't look good, but give me some time. I'm going to do some digging and see what I can find out."

Karen called the USW lawyer representing the retirees' court case. He took the position that Century was likely within their rights to use the funds for their own reimbursement. The president of the USW retiree organization, SOAR (Steelworkers Organization for Active Retirees), talked with his lawyers and told Karen they had come to the same conclusion.

Unfortunately, Century was likely not acting illegally or outside the intended scope of use for the funds. Karen wasn't convinced. That evening she sat at her computer where she would remain through the night and all of the following day. She found a copy of the rules and regulations for the ERRP and read and reread every line looking for evidence to prove that Century was in the wrong.

The ERRP provided companies with options for how they use the funds. Employers could choose to reduce their plans' expenses by receiving reimbursements for eligible medical claims submitted by retirees. They could also pass the savings on to retirees by reimbursing them for their insurance premiums. Still, Karen believed Century was taking too much leeway. She made her case to Senators Jay Rockefeller's and Joe Manchin's offices in Washington in a three-page email, where she included specific text from the regulations supporting her conclusion that Century's planned use of funds did not comply with ERRP regulations. She argued broadly that their plan went against the program's intended outcome of providing affordable health insurance options for early retirees. Both Senators Rockefeller and Manchin agreed to investigate the situation further, and Karen kept in contact with both offices, not willing to give up on this effort.

US senator John Davidson (Jay) Rockefeller IV, great-grandson of the famed industrialist and philanthropist John D. Rockefeller, was born in New York City, attended Harvard University, studied in Japan, and worked in Washington, DC, before landing in the small community of Emmons, West Virginia, in 1964. Emmons sits along the Big Coal River, twenty-some miles from Charleston. At the time of Jay's arrival, the town was five miles from the nearest paved road and home to fewer than 100 families. The twenty-seven-year-old Rockefeller arrived in Emmons to work a two-year term as an AmeriCorps VISTA Volunteer. (VISTA is a domestic volunteer program modeled after the Peace Corps.) In time, Jay Rockefeller would put down roots, earning the trust of his new community in Emmons, then his congressional district, and then the state. After his VISTA stint, in 1967, Rockefeller began his political career as representative in the West Virginia House of Delegates and, two years later, as West Virginia's secretary of state. He served as West Virginia's governor from 1977 to 1985, when he began his first term as a US senator. When Century Aluminum retirees lost their insurance, Rockefeller was serving his fifth term in that office.

Karen and Senator Rockefeller had met briefly, in 1979, at Karen's father's funeral. His appearance was a surprise to Karen, who had not realized her father knew or had made an impression on the then governor. The fact that Rockefeller had paid his respects to her father made a lasting impression on Karen, however, and she had a deep respect for the man. Rockefeller's office had already been pressing Century to use its ERRP funding to extend insurance coverage for retirees, Karen learned. Senator Rockefeller wrote to Century CEO Logan Kruger in December 2010 expressing his concern that Century had decided to drop retiree insurance plans despite the financial assistance from the ERRP. He urged Century to reconsider, noting that the loss of insurance could negatively impact retirees' economic well-being, especially those living with chronic conditions. "Standing by your workers during this time in their lives is simply the right thing to do," he argued. Rockefeller continued to send letters and even called Kruger to discuss the issue, but to no avail. Century informed the senator that the ERRP funds, in its opinion, did not go far enough.

By February 2011, Rockefeller turned to the Obama administration for support, meeting with US labor secretary Hilda

Solis to share his concerns and work toward a solution to prevent similar occurrences. He knew that the Ravenswood retirees were not the only Americans to believe that their retirement benefits would continue for their lifetime, despite employers' decisions to end them. Worse, courts were upholding the companies' decisions, giving others the green light to follow suit. In his letter to Solis, Rockefeller advocated for better benefits disclosure requirements so that employees would not be misled into believing that benefits were guaranteed for their lifetime, while employers quietly reserved the right to terminate them. Details such as these should be explicit and open for discussion during contract negotiations, he wrote.

Wes Holden routinely forwarded Karen press releases from Rockefeller's office to keep her informed of their efforts on the retirees' behalf. In turn, Karen kept Wes informed of the retirees' work. She knew that having his and Rockefeller's commitment to the retirees' cause was not inconsequential. She also came to see Wes as not just an ally but also a friend and would turn to him for advice and for hope when she was running low. Wes, an army veteran and a tenth-generation West Virginian, started working for Senator Rockefeller in 1985. He took pride in working on behalf of West Virginians, and he believed in Karen's campaign. He saw something of himself in Karen's dedication to her cause, and her refusal to be told that she couldn't do something. The two of them clicked, and he thought nothing of going beyond what his job required to support her.

Wes agreed with those who had given Karen the nickname "Momma K," in a nod to her similarities with Mother Jones, the iconic labor organizer of the late nineteenth and early twentieth centuries. Mary Harris, who would become known as Mother Jones, earned a reputation fighting for and with

7, 2011, at the Hyatt Regency Hotel in Monterey, California. An invitation had just arrived in the mail. By owning shares in Century Aluminum Company common stock, Mike Gorrell was invited to attend as a voting member. Most likely, Mike received a similar letter in the mail every year for the last twenty years or more. Most likely, he had thrown them in the trash.

The retirees had been discussing the possibility of traveling to California to address Century's management for months, and Karen knew this was their chance. There was just one catch: Karen wasn't a shareholder, so she could only attend if her husband, Mike, also went. Mike didn't take well to flying and didn't care much for traveling in general. Karen knew there would be no sense in trying to talk him into starting now. Plus, Karen had accepted that this fight was her calling, not his. Mike Gorrell was content living a quiet life, remaining in the background. He was not a big talker, avoided crowds, and certainly did not wear his heart on his sleeve, as Karen did. He was, however, deeply devoted to Karen and his family. He provided for them. That was how he showed love. He worked a lot—regularly volunteering for double shifts for the overtime pay. Or he took on side jobs in his time off. He was meticulous about routine maintenance on their vehicles and their home. Now retired, he stayed busy with projects and odd jobs and found new ways to be useful, seeing to it that his loved ones' lives were comfortable. Mike and Karen's son, Chad, might roll his eyes occasionally when Mike picked up the grandkids at the bus stop so they didn't have to walk the quarter mile in a drizzle of rain—Chad had simply walked in the rain at that age—but he appreciated his dad's dedication and admired his dad for stepping up and taking over as the primary babysitter for Chad's two children, now that Karen was hyperfocused on the campaign for health benefits.

There was a group of retirees and spouses meeting regularly now, and like Karen, they were committed to take any action they could to further their cause. The group included Ron and Betty Dixon, who had driven the group caravan to Cleveland in April. Ron had short gray hair, kind eyes, and a sincere smile. He had grown up in Jackson County and hired on at the plant as a welder in 1976 and then worked as a millwright, retiring in 2005. Many who worked with Ron knew him by his nickname, Ripcord. A parachute and BASE jumper by hobby, Ripcord was a regular at West Virginia's annual Bridge Day event, where he and dozens of others launched themselves from the iconic New River Gorge Bridge with nothing but a parachute and prayer guiding them to the rocks and water below. He would make that leap thirty-four times during his life and log twenty-three hundred parachute jumps between 1968 and 2010. The retirees knew Ripcord was comfortable taking a risk and would be someone who could keep his cool under pressure. So Ripcord was nominated to be Karen's stand-in husband at the shareholders' meeting. Everyone agreed that Karen should be the one to address the board of directors, and having Ripcord pretend to be her husband was their plan to get her inside the meeting room.

Ripcord and Karen would also be joined by "Gibby" Adkins and John Morris. John had retired from Century Aluminum in 2002, at the same time as Jim Weltner. John was in good health now, though he had bypass surgery in 2004. He had done his research afterward and took steps to change his diet in hopes of preventing another. Now, he took a similar approach toward the retirees' cause, hoping that if he and the others could sort out how this had been allowed to happen to them, they could work to prevent it from happening to others through legal or legislative action.

John had moved to Jackson County from a small town in Boone County, about thirty miles south of Charleston. He attended elementary school in a two-room schoolhouse, worked as a paperboy throughout his youth, and helped his uncle run the small town's post office before marrying and starting a family. Then like so many other young men from the coalfields at the time, John left southern West Virginia in search of work, landing a job with Kaiser Aluminum in 1964. He was twenty-five years old, with two young boys still at home with his wife, Mary. John was grateful to be settling in West Virginia, after traveling as far as Connecticut to follow a lead on a construction job. Though jobs farther north, even those at auto plants in Ohio, may have paid better, Kaiser's plant offered excellent pay and benefits for the region, which for John, was home.

The night before Karen and her crew would fly to California, Mike Gorrell called John Morris, Gibby Adkins, and Ripcord. He asked each of them to promise that they would look after Karen on their trip. They did. It had surprised Karen a little that Mike didn't try to talk her out of going or that it hadn't led to a big argument. She thought of their arguments about her going back to work once the kids were in school. They didn't need the money. It just seemed right to him that Karen would be at home. But he came around, then, and he certainly knew by now, after more than thirty years together, that when Karen set her mind to something, you'd run out of breath trying to talk her out of it. Fighting for the retirees was Karen's work, and people Mike had known and worked with for decades were looking to her for leadership.

The next evening, in Monterey, California, Karen sat at the edge of the bed in her hotel room, wondering if she would be able to sleep that night in the unfamiliar space. There was so much more noise filtering in from the city than she was used to. Karen's thoughts turned to Bryce Turner, who should have been with them. He had wanted to make the trip. Instead, he lay in a hospital bed at Cleveland Clinic, having been admitted the week prior. Before leaving, Karen told Bryce to focus on his recovery, and she would take care of Century. She asked Bryce's wife for a headshot of Bryce, which she had printed on a neon yellow T-shirt, surrounded by the following text:

> Bryce Turner Has Acute Myelogenous Leukemia
>
> In Century Aluminum's effort to ensure profit, they are terminating his promised retiree health care after years of his dedicated service
>
> *Murder without a Gun*

Karen's cell phone rang, interrupting her thoughts. Her accomplices, Ripcord, John, and Gibby, were on the other line. They had been talking, and they didn't think her wearing the T-shirt with Bryce's photo was a good idea. It was too provocative, and they couldn't risk being asked to leave before she had a chance to speak. Karen knew it was a risk, but she was willing to take it.

"Look, if you don't want to go in with me, I'll understand. But I told Bryce I would bring him to this shareholders' meeting, and that's what I'm gonna do."

The next day, Ripcord, now "Mike Gorrell," managed to get into the shareholders' meeting without showing any identification. Karen showed her ID at the desk, and when she saw the woman looking expectantly at Ripcord, hand extended, Karen asked her husband, making herself sound irritated, if he had left his wallet in the hotel room. "I must have," he said, pretending to search his pockets. It was good enough, though it wasn't his only close call. Before the meeting began, Karen took advantage of an opportunity to speak with Century's communication officer in person. Karen had hoped for this moment, as she had a lot she wanted to say after reading a press statement in which he had referred to the retirees' loss of insurance as "unfortunate."

"Accidents are unfortunate," Karen told him, "and what Century did was no accident." Karen spent the next several minutes spelling out the wrongs the company had committed. "What's unfortunate," Karen said, "is how much these men have sacrificed, only to be kicked to the curb." She was talking about dedicated employees, she told him, "Like my husband. He lost part of his finger in an accident at the plant. He was rushed off to surgery and he still came back to finish his shift that night," she blurted out, catching herself after it was too late. *Shit*, she thought. Her "husband" was standing nearby with the other retirees, with all ten fingers intact. Ripcord, "Mike Gorrell," calmly put his left hand in his pocket and made a mental note to keep it there for the rest of the day.

Inside the meeting room, Karen took her seat next to her "husband" and looked at Century's board of directors seated at the front of the room. She thought about the advice someone from the union had given her. "Don't be surprised if they don't look at you. They're going to act like you're wasting their time," she had been told. They ended the pep talk, which was not very encouraging, by saying, "You can't shame corporate America." Karen's heart began to race. She wasn't going to make a difference, she thought. This was foolish. Then she thought of the hundreds of families in Jackson County, all counting on her to get this right. *You can do this, Karen*, she repeated to herself, until she heard her name called. She could feel the sweat on her palms and her brow and the sting of tears threatening to let loose. *Dear Lord, please, help me get through this*, she prayed.

"Mrs. Gorrell, we understand you have a few words to share," someone said. "Please stand." The room turned toward Karen. It was silent. She stood, shaking a little, not sure if her legs were going to hold her.

"Yes, thank you," she managed to begin, feeling incredibly nervous. She studied her audience. They did look bored, just like she had been told. But she had to make this moment count. Karen was sure that Century's board of directors had not considered the West Virginia retirees beyond the money they represented on the company's books, and she told them so. Until today, perhaps, the Ravenswood retirees were just a line item on a spreadsheet, "an 'X' in a box," she said. So she had come, from West Virginia, to introduce Century's board of directors to some of the retirees affected by Century's decisions.

"I'm sure each of you has a wife, a son, a daughter, a sibling—people in your life who love you very much and who would like to see you live for as long as you can," Karen said, finding her confidence. The board members' eyes were fixed on her now. "And so do we," she said, looking to the retirees beside her. "We are real people, with beating hearts, just like you."

Karen spoke about Sam McKinney, how he cut back his heart medication before dying of a heart attack. She then held out the bottom of her T-shirt so that Bryce's face was clearly visible. "Bryce Turner couldn't be here today to meet you because he is lying in a hospital bed on the other side of the country. Fighting for his life. But I want you to remember this man's face. As long as you live, I want you to remember Bryce Turner. He gave thirty-six and a half years of his life at your Ravenswood plant, and he deserves better than to be fighting cancer while counting down the days until he loses the health insurance that he worked hard for and was promised by your company." She was emotional but saw that the men's eyes were still on her. "Every single time you pull up to the bank with your fat profits check, I want you to remember what your decisions are doing to this man in West Virginia." She started to take her seat, then straightened, taking a moment to look at the face of each man seated in front of her. "Shame on you," she added.

Seated again, Karen took a minute to compose herself and steady her breathing. The next thing she knew, Century's board members were filing out of their seats and through the exit door. Only the CEO, Logan Kruger, and board president, John O'Brien, stopped to shake the retirees' hands. Karen explained to Mr. Kruger that they had traveled a long way, and she wondered if he could spare thirty minutes of his time to meet with them. He declined and exited the room.

Back in West Virginia, at the next retiree meeting Karen passed around a photo album from the California trip, showing her, John, Gibby, and Ripcord smiling in front of the Pacific Ocean, wearing their signature "Our Blood Is on Century's Hands" T-shirts. In one photo, Ripcord holds up his hand, ring finger bent to look like it was half missing. He'd repeatedly given Karen a hard time about that slip-up, and the story got a good laugh from the retirees at home.

There were also photos of the retirees picketing outside of Century's office building with members of the California Alliance of Retired Americans (CARA), a connection made by the USW SOAR president. CARA had sent out an email to their members to show up to the Century retirees' picket, and Karen reported that she was amazed at the support they encountered from complete strangers. She had to admit that she had no idea if her speech had any impact on Century's board members, but she could see the impact their story had on working people, especially fellow union members. If the Ravenswood retirees alone couldn't persuade Century to do the right thing, they would have to keep traveling and picketing until they had enough supporters to make a difference.

In the meantime, Karen said, there was new business to attend to. So far, the retirees had mostly paid for their travel expenses out of pocket. For the trip to California, though, they received a $2,000 donation from SOAR, and nearly $2,000 more from a bucket drive the retirees had organized at the entrance to the Constellium rolling facility, which sat next to the Century plant. Constellium workers were also represented by the USW, and they took note of what was going on with Century's retirees, understanding they could be the next in line to lose their benefits.

"I think we should open a checking account for donations," Karen suggested. "I can make arrangements to set it up, but I don't want to be the only one responsible for this money. We should see that each check is signed by two retirees, and we should nominate people who can access the account, like a committee."

It made sense, and right away, someone suggested nominating those who traveled to California: Karen, John Morris, Ripcord Dixon, and Gibby Adkins. The only dissenting point was that Gibby now lived in Cincinnati, so someone else suggested Jim Weltner, who lived near Karen in Mineral Wells. Then someone said that a committee should have an odd number of members as a tiebreaker in case of a vote, and Les Shockey was nominated as the fifth person. Les had already committed substantial time and effort to the retirees' cause. He had set up and now managed the Century Aluminum retirees' website, where he shared and archived photos, listed important updates, and kept a running memorial page for retirees who had passed away since they had started their campaign. He was also not new to organizing. Like all of the retirees working closely with Karen, Les was a veteran of the lockout, having served as a picket captain and as part of the communications team. An amateur radio operator, he had built the radio antennae for the union's picket shacks and installed scanners at the union hall to monitor communication in the plant. He was good, designing quarter-wave antennae for the portable radios that reached farther than the walkie-talkies they had access to.

Les had retired from the plant in 2006 after more than forty-three years on the job. He had suffered a stroke since retirement but was still active and committed to fighting Century. He knew the union had bargained for retiree health care for as long as there had been a union. He knew that workers retired during the lockout because retirement offered health insurance benefits for life. He knew that what Century did was wrong, and he wasn't willing to stand by and let the company get away with it.

Those present at the retiree meeting voted to approve the nominations: Karen Gorrell, John Morris, Ron "Ripcord" Dixon, Jim Weltner, and Les Shockey. With that, the Century Aluminum retirees now had a committee to represent them.

Chapter Five

When you are in these desperate situations, you truly realize what a union means—united as one and together forever!
—Karen Gorrell

Promises: June 2011

As the excitement over the retirees' California trip quieted, rumors about the plant's closure began to pick up. It made the local papers: Century could be putting the Ravenswood plant up for sale. The journal *American Metal Market* first published the story, speculating that three companies could each have their eye on the plant. The article noted that the ongoing lawsuit and the lack of a power contract weren't going to sweeten the deal for a potential buyer, but each of the three companies would have something to gain from the purchase. Plus, it appeared that any of Century's assets were potentially for sale for the right price. The article quoted a US analyst as saying, "Century can't publicly say they're not committed to [the Ravenswood plant] if they're ever going to get a decent power deal there, but I think they're going to say they're committed to it until they're not."

Karen wondered if the news was connected to the fact that Century had voted in three new board members at the June shareholders' meeting. Initially, Karen had been optimistic, hearing that one of the new members, Terence Wilkinson, would replace O'Brien as chair. It had been just two months since the retirees had visited O'Brien's home. Karen thought the end of his term might not be a coincidence and took it as a sign that they were getting through to Century. Unfortunately, the *Charleston Gazette-Mail* reported that the three new board members were Glencore representatives (the company still owned more than 40 percent of Century's stock). Given Ravenswood's history with Glencore during the lockout, Karen and others worried that the company's increased presence on Century's board wasn't a good sign for retirees.

If Century permanently closed the plant, the retirees would lose their leverage in negotiations. But there still might be a way forward, Karen hoped. She had written a letter to a respected local attorney, who responded that they believed the retirees could file a class action suit alleging age discrimination. Karen forwarded this letter to the Office of the West Virginia Attorney General, asking for advice. Chief Deputy Attorney General Frances Hughes responded that there was a good likelihood that they could have a class action certified, and that this may be one of the best routes for the retirees to pursue, if it were feasible for them to pursue this option. Karen was wary of how long a court case could take to resolve. She also had more immediate matters to attend to. With less than a month until Century's payments for their COBRA (Consolidated Omnibus Budget Reconciliation Act) insurance premiums expired, Karen kept her attention focused on protesting Century's use of their Early Retiree Reinsurance Program (ERRP) funding.

In June 2011, the governor's office called Karen's cell phone, requesting a meeting. *Well, what do you know*, Karen thought. Governor Earl Ray Tomblin had been in his current office for six months, yet the retirees' repeated attempts to secure a meeting had been unproductive. Recently, Karen had gone as far as to announce that the retirees were planning to protest on the Capitol grounds until the governor agreed to see them. By now it was becoming clear to anyone paying attention—journalists and politicians included—that Karen wasn't one to bluff, and it seemed her message about the planned protest had gotten through to its intended audience. "Don't bother with the overnight bags," Karen told the group planning to travel with her to Charleston. "This trip won't be nearly as long as we thought. It seems the governor has found some time for us."

On Wednesday, June 22, 2011, Karen and several retirees sat down for their first meeting with Governor Tomblin and state commerce secretary Keith Burdette. The retirees knew that Tomblin had supported the Century bill that had stalled in the legislature that spring. But they also knew he had not yet heard from them directly, and they wanted to give him that opportunity. In their conversation, Karen reiterated that while the retirees wanted the Ravenswood plant to reopen, they could not understand how anyone in good conscience could allow Century to restart the plant without paying its dues to retirees. She reminded the governor that Century was not a bankrupt company. In fact, she said, terminating retirees' health plans boosted its profits by $11.5 million in the first quarter of the year. This was a company that valued profits more than it valued the lives of those who labored in its plants.

"Is that really the kind of company that we want to do business with in West Virginia?" she asked.

Governor Tomblin assured Karen that he would keep the retirees' concerns in mind. There had been no discussions between his office and Century regarding the Century bill since last January, he noted. Should talk resume, he would strongly encourage Century to reconsider its decision to terminate health-care benefits. And he assured the retirees that they would have a seat at the table. The governor thanked them for their visit and asked, as a farewell formality, if there was anything else that he could do to assist them. Karen stood and paused for a moment, not wanting to waste this opportunity. She took a breath before meeting the governor's eye.

"Well, sir, yes, there is one more thing you can do for us," Karen said. The others remained seated, watching her. "I want you to get your tush," she said, sternly, "out of that cushy little chair and walk out that door and tell the media waiting outside that you have our backs." Karen's companions stared at her in disbelief. Her arm was outstretched, her hand pointing at the door. "Because with all respect, Governor," she said, "you can tell us anything you want here in this office and then forget about it tomorrow. But if you tell the media, we'll know you really support us."

Tomblin agreed to speak with reporters, and the next day, journalist Jared Hunt published an article for the *Charleston Gazette-Mail* outlining the governor's meeting with retirees and his stance on Century Aluminum: if the company wanted to discuss electricity rates, it should also be prepared to talk about retiree health insurance.

As the end of June approached and retirees anxiously anticipated the end of their COBRA insurance benefits, Senator Jay Rockefeller sent a new round of letters stressing his concern with Century's decision not to use the available ERRP funding to extend retiree benefits. He wrote to Century CEO Logan Kruger, US labor secretary Hilda Solis, Department of Health and Human Services (HHS) secretary Kathleen Sebelius, and Securities and Exchange Commission chair Mary Schapiro. Wes Holden, with Rockefeller's office, had also set up a video conference for the newly formed Retiree Committee with the Department of Health and Human Services. On the call, Karen pleaded her case. She discussed the conclusions she had drawn regarding Century's use of the ERRP funds, and emphasized that retirees' lives were at stake.

Senator Joe Manchin had also written to Secretary Sebelius over the summer, and the response his office forwarded to Karen offered the retirees little encouragement. As others had done, the secretary explained that Century was likely justified in its use of ERRP funds and was under no obligation to extend insurance coverage for retirees. In spite of the repeated dissuasions, however, Karen would learn that her persistence, in the final hour, had paid off. On June 28, 2010, just two days before Century's payments for retiree COBRA premiums were set to expire, Karen emailed a couple dozen retirees to let them know she had spoken with someone at the COBRA administration office: Century had changed its position. The company would extend its coverage of COBRA premiums for retirees, who would receive a letter with details in the coming days.

"Finally," Karen wrote, "after all the hard work, the letter writing, the hours in front of a computer . . . the grandmas and grandpas could put one down on the winning side of the score sheet." She had refused to accept Century's line of reasoning, and her persistence, she believed, had bought them this extra time. It was exactly the win they needed to boost morale, even if the details weren't ideal. Retirees would have to elect individually to continue COBRA coverage and pay the costly premiums upfront. Worse, Century was only committing to reimbursements for the month of July and maybe August if funds remained available. But as Karen would tell the retirees, "That's two months I can have a heart attack and afford to see a doctor."

The news left Karen feeling a mix of relief and disappointment. She told retirees in her email, "I pray this is the beginning of the total resolution of this battle, but one never knows what is on their minds. We must continue the battle until

Karen speaks from the podium at the Fort Unity stage in Ravenswood.

justice is won." She knew this meant Bryce Turner could continue to pay for his medications and treatment without stress for at least another month, and she was grateful for that, even though it made her sick to think of what would happen afterward. Bryce wasn't doing well, she knew. After a six-week stay at Cleveland Clinic, he was released home only to end up back in the hospital weeks later.

Fort Unity: July 2011–September 2011

Century did reimburse retirees for COBRA premiums through August 2011. Still, the clock was ticking, and the retirees wanted to send a clear message that they weren't backing down as Century continued to profit at their expense. A July press release from the company announced quarterly profits were up $8.9 million as a result of "changes to the Century of West Virginia retiree medical benefits program." The "changes" also added "an associated discrete tax benefit of $2.1 million."

The retirees kept busy. They were preparing to "reopen Fort Unity," the nickname of the Ravenswood union hall during the lockout. "One Day More . . . Again!" was the retirees' slogan this time around, a nod to the labor song "One Day More" written by Elaine Purkey about the Ravenswood lockout. The rally was scheduled for August 27, 2011, and retirees spent July and August planning the event. It would include a potluck meal with speakers and bands at the outdoor stage next to the union hall.

Retirees and volunteers held cleanup days to give Fort Unity a needed facelift. They cleaned, made minor repairs, and mounted a new sign above the stage reading "Century has hung its retirees out for slaughter!" with an effigy of a retiree hanging from the roof. The project brought the retirees together, and it brought back memories. For some, the lockout had been one of the more challenging experiences they had lived through. It also was an experience that many looked back on with pride. They were older now, which the work on Fort Unity reminded them of, but they were just as committed to this cause. Though after burying more than a dozen retirees in just the past year, they understood that none of them knew how much time they had left.

Karen spent her days working on logistics, including lining up speakers and inviting the group's growing list of supporters. She sent invitations to other locals of the United Steelworkers Union (USW), from Hawesville, Kentucky, to Marietta, Ohio. Several locals responded with encouragement and monetary donations. Unions near and far remembered the lockout, and the reputation of USW Local 5668 in Ravenswood was well established. Karen's list also included Governor Tomblin, Senators Rockefeller and Manchin, West Virginia secretary of state Natalie Tennant, several West Virginia legislators, West Virginia attorney general Darrell McGraw, and contacts from the AFL-CIO (American Federation of Labor and Congress of Industrial Organizations), the Alliance for Retired Americans (ARA) West Virginia chapter, and the Communication Workers of America (CWA). Elaine Harris, international staff representative with the CWA, had become someone the retirees could count on. As a woman who dedicated her career to advocating for workers, she made herself available when Karen reached out for advice.

Despite the broad support and encouragement Karen received, she was not always sure where she stood with the USW. She continued to communicate, but she had mostly given up on asking for direction or guidance. She was informing now: of events she and the retirees planned or courses of action she wanted to pursue.

Leading up to the rally on August 10, 2011, Karen received a phone call from SOAR (Steelworkers Organization for Active Retirees) director Jim Centner. He followed up with an email. There had been some concern that the Fort Unity rally was presenting the wrong message about reopening the Ravenswood plant. The slogan *No Healthcare, No Startup* was problematic. He reminded Karen that the best hope for restoring retiree benefits was for Century to restart the plant so the union had an avenue for bargaining on the retirees' behalf. Century, Centner told Karen, was trying to run a business, and the retirees couldn't embarrass the company. Karen was shocked. Later that evening, she put out a call to the Retiree Committee.

"John, we need to meet. I'm not going to be able to sleep tonight if I don't tell you all what just happened."

"I'll be there," he responded.

Karen lit a cigarette as she got into her car and backed out of the driveway. "Who is embarrassing who, Jim?" she said out loud to herself as she turned onto the dark two-lane road and headed toward the highway. "This is the union's contract that the company is walking all over." As she replayed the conversation in her head, she felt angry and uneasy. She and John and the others sat in a booth at the McDonald's just off the highway in Ravenswood, where Karen shared an account of her conversation. The group discussed how to respond, though Karen had already been drafting a reply in her head.

The following day, the retirees made a planned trip to Hawesville, Kentucky, a six-hour drive, to drum up support for the Fort Unity rally. The event was a great success and helped remind Karen that there was an outpouring of support for their cause. They were doing the right thing. Still, her thoughts kept circling back to her conversation with Centner. That evening, once she felt like she had collected herself enough to do so, she sat down at her computer.

"Embarrassing Century is the least of our worries," she wrote in her three-page email. "Embarrassing is when your doctor asks you how you intend to pay for your bill, and you can't answer. Embarrassing is when, after decades of working and saving, you have to decline outings with friends and family because your entire pension is being spent on health insurance premiums." Karen outlined the retirees' campaign successes, noting how they'd become a topic of conversation in major arenas throughout the state. Without the retirees taking action, their plight would have been out of the news and out of everyone's mind last December. She reiterated that the retirees had no intention of sabotaging efforts to restart the plant, but they stood firm in their belief that the plant should not restart without Century honoring existing obligations to retirees. "How can the union sit down and negotiate with Century in good faith, knowing they've made a mockery of past contracts?" she asked, adding, "Century has no problem embarrassing the union and convincing judges that it is the union's fault we are in this position."

Karen wrote that the union's strategies during the lockout inspired her approach to this campaign. Those two years proved that grit and dedication could pay off when you're fighting on the right side of history. The lockout was the battle that saved the union, she knew, because the union was willing to take bold action and to toss the rule book aside. The way she remembered it, embarrassing the opponent *was* the strategy. How else could you justify the larger-than-life puppet of Glencore CEO Marc Rich being paraded through the streets of Europe? The union wanted to attract attention to the fugitive billionaire's role in keeping hundreds of West Virginia families from earning a paycheck, because they needed leverage to bring the company to the bargaining table. If the strategy had worked once, she questioned, why abandon it now? "The retirees do not have the resources the International had to go to those extremes," she noted, "but I assure you that if we could, we would."

Centner let Karen know that he planned to attend the rally and wanted to confirm that they were on the same page: the event would be about benefits and jobs, the union and its retirees working together on behalf of all those disenfranchised by Century. Although Centner assured her that they were fighting on the same side, it was becoming clear to Karen that they had different approaches.

The week before the Fort Unity rally, the Fourth US Circuit Court of Appeals ruled on the retirees' case and upheld the lower court's decision to deny the union's request for a preliminary injunction. As a result, Century would not be required to maintain the retirees' health insurance plans while the case was tried. It was another vote of no confidence, though Karen wasn't surprised. She and a group of retirees had attended the hearing in May, driving to Richmond, Virginia, for the occasion. She had left disappointed.

The USW lawyer representing the retirees argued that when it came to contract language, particularly pertaining to benefits, one needed to consider the context. This had already been established, he claimed, quoting: "The intended meaning of even the most explicit language can only be understood in light of the context which gives rise to its inclusion." He argued, like the retirees would argue, that this was common sense: retiree benefits were implicitly understood to last throughout a person's retirement, not just for a few years.

"It's not ambiguous," he said, adding, "The agreements are replete with forward-looking promises of activity which will take place after the expiration of the agreements, thus suggesting that the parties' intent was that the benefits would continue beyond expiration."

Century's lawyers argued that unlike pensions, which were described as "fully vested" in the contract, retiree benefits were described using durational language—they continued only for the duration of the contract.

It was a tense six-hour drive back to Ravenswood.

"They didn't even let him speak!" Karen said to her companions. "Century's lawyers got to do all the talking." She felt frustrated at the repeated interruptions during the hearing and frustrated that what she and every other retiree knew to be true could be misconstrued in a court of law. "This system is broken," Karen vented. "If these cases were really decided fairly, it wouldn't matter where you filed your case. But it does! That's why the steelworkers filed in Ohio. In the end, all that matters is the judge's politics. The facts don't matter at all." She sat silent for a while. "Jim, I'm sorry, but you're gonna have to stop. If I don't smoke a cigarette I might explode."

Losing the appeal was difficult news, but for Karen it validated her decision not to back down in her efforts. *This is going to be up to us, not the courts*, she told herself.

On the day of the rally, August 27, 2011, Karen's core group—her "retiree army," as she called them—arrived early to help set up for the event. By early afternoon dozens of supporters had arrived, including a bus of union workers from the Century Aluminum plant in Hawesville, Kentucky. The trip was organized by the USW Local 9423 president John Beaver, who would become an important ally for the retirees in Ravenswood.

It lifted Karen's heart to see such a large turnout at the event. Her father had taught her the value of the union, and she thought she knew what he meant, having lived through the

Bryce Turner speaks to a reporter at the retirees' rally in Charleston.

lockout. This was different, though, now that she was leading the charge. *This is what a union looks like,* she said to herself, scanning the crowd before she took the stage. In her speech, Karen reminded the audience that many retirees were too sick or too frail to join this fight. She was grateful for those who were standing up and showing up in their place. She thanked the politicians who believed in the retirees and all those who traveled to be a part of this event. She knew that many guests, like those from Hawesville, came with the understanding that they could one day face the same fate as Ravenswood. Others were here because they had already lived through the challenges the Ravenswood retirees were now facing.

West Virginia attorney general Darrell McGraw, seventy-five years old, had served as attorney general in West Virginia since 1992 and planned to run the following year for another term. He was the first attorney general in the US to sue Purdue Pharma over its marketing practices for the opioid drug OxyContin, back in 2001. At the Fort Unity rally, McGraw told reporters that his office was investigating the retirees' case. He believed the retirees when they claimed their labor contracts protected their benefits, and he hoped to offer his support.

Washington: September 2011

On September 1, 2011, Karen got the call she had been dreading. Bryce Turner was not doing well. She should come to see him. That evening, she stood for a moment in the hallway outside of his hospital room, working up the courage to go inside. She wasn't ready to say goodbye, and she hated knowing that after all their effort, it had still come to this. Their health-care subsidies were ending, and yet there was no end in sight for their campaign and no reprieve from the health conditions that plagued so many retirees. Karen chatted for a while with Bryce and his wife, Cindy. It pained her to see Bryce looking so weak. Yet he was still so calm and so kindhearted in spite of everything. Karen eventually said she should be going. Bryce asked her to come sit next to him.

"You're the gutsiest woman I've ever met, Karen, and I am so proud of you," he said to her. It was hard for her to speak then. "Come here, give me a hug," he said. Karen had tried to hold back her tears while with him, but his words went right to her heart.

"Bryce," Karen said, when she composed herself, "I'm not going to stop until we get our health insurance back. Whatever happens, I want you to know that. I'm going to see this through to the end. I promise you. If I have breath left in my body, I'm going to fight this, so we can take care of Cindy, OK?"

The next day, on September 2, Karen learned that Bryce Turner had died from complications from leukemia. Since his diagnosis, he had been through two rounds of chemotherapy in the Cleveland Clinic and another five rounds at a hospital in Parkersburg, West Virginia.

Karen was heartbroken. She felt physically ill. She thought of all the disappointment, stress, and anger that had fueled her efforts for nine months. So far, Century had relented just two months of health insurance, and now that coverage, too, had expired. Still, knowing that Bryce had health insurance until his finals days was worth every ounce of effort. Karen had not given up and had persisted in making her case, even when she felt like the only voice speaking up. She told herself that if she hadn't taken this on, Century would not have changed course, and Bryce would have spent his final days uninsured. *Rest in peace, dear friend,* Karen spoke to him in prayer that evening. *We will battle on.*

Karen grieved Bryce's death, but she didn't slow down. She didn't have time. On September 6, she and a group of eight retirees and spouses planned to travel to Washington, DC, where Karen would speak about the Ravenswood retirees' battle for health-care benefits at the ARA Tenth Annual Celebration and Legislative Conference. The event would welcome ARA members from more than one thousand chapters across the country. It would also be the first time Karen addressed a national audience, something she had hoped to achieve for months.

Throughout the summer, Karen discussed plans for the event with her ARA contacts, the two women who welcomed the retirees and stood beside them when they took their campaign to California. She confirmed details over email in mid-July. The next steps were to finalize plans for Senator Rockefeller and Senator Manchin to introduce Karen before her speech.

As the event neared, Karen reached out to her contact at the ARA to clarify details, and received a devastating update: she was not listed as a speaker on the agenda.

Panic overwhelmed Karen for a moment. "What do you mean?" was all she could manage to say. Then she looked at the papers she had gathered in front of her and picked up a sticky note attached to the event brochure. On it, she had written "USW Delegate Breakfast—Thursday, 7 a.m." Karen sighed. She explained that recently there had been some disagreements between the retirees and the union. The two sides didn't always agree about Karen's messaging.

Still grieving the loss of Bryce, Karen moved through the week in a daze, unable to get her bearings. What frustrated her was that the speech she had planned was not just about Ravenswood. She hoped to use the situation in Ravenswood to encourage retirees across the country to demand national legislation to stop the theft of benefits from retirees. Knowing that Senator Rockefeller and Senator Manchin supported this effort, she wanted to build on that momentum. This could be a national movement. They could stop this from happening again. At 4:00 a.m., Karen looked at the alarm clock next to her bed. She was still awake, her thoughts circling, when she made her decision. Later that morning, just two days before the event, she called her companions.

"We need to go to DC. We might not be on stage, but that doesn't mean we can't show up and handbill every person at that conference." She already had the handbills ready.

When the Ravenswood retirees arrived at the Hilton Hotel, Karen was surprised to see a familiar face in the lobby, a retiree from the Special Metals plant in Marietta, Ohio, who had attended the Fort Unity rally. He recognized Karen right away and told her he couldn't wait to see her take the stage.

"Look, I'm not going to be on stage," Karen informed him. She laid out a short version of recent events and her speculation as to why she wasn't on the agenda. The retiree was upset, and he didn't hide it. *I haven't been here but five minutes, and I've already opened a can of worms,* Karen thought, as this man carried on, causing a scene inside the hotel. When her phone rang, she excused herself and walked outside through the front doors of the hotel, shaking her head. She wanted to bring attention to the Ravenswood retirees, it was true, but not like this. She answered her phone.

It was Senator Manchin's office, asking to verify the time of her speech. She hadn't spoken to his office in the past week, she realized. Then she had to break the news again.

Later that afternoon Karen was back in front of the hotel, smoking a cigarette. As she watched the stream of cars and pedestrians, she thought about the opportunity she was missing out on and felt her anger brewing. Ripcord came outside then, interrupting her thoughts.

"Well, Jim knows we're here," he said. "He's not very happy about this guy from Special Metals running his mouth. He said he had tickets for us for some fancy dinner tonight, but he wasn't giving them to us now."

"Of course he isn't," said Karen. "That's what he seems to be good at, holding out promises and taking them away when he thinks we're out of line." She put out her cigarette and turned to face Ripcord. "I'd rather eat a cold McDonald's hamburger than sit down to dinner with that man right now."

Several retirees, including Ripcord and Betty Dixon and John and Mary Morris, were in the lobby with Karen while she spoke with Centner and one of his colleagues the next day. The retirees had spent the morning working in shifts at the entrance to the hotel, passing out the handbill that described their situation to everyone who entered.

"Why were we pulled from the agenda?" Karen asked without hiding her anger. The conversation was heated. Even Mary and Betty, who always kept their cool, became visibly upset, raising their voices. Eventually the hotel security guard moved in the group's direction, signaling that the conversation needed to quiet down or end. Before it did, Centner's colleague let the retirees know where they stood.

"I want to tell you now," he said, "you may think you're doing big things, but without the union, you're not going to get anywhere."

Chapter Six

We may have one foot in the grave, but
we can still kick with the other.

—Karen Gorrell

Departure: September 2011–December 2011

In November 2011, Karen returned home after running errands and went to her office to check her email before cooking dinner. She had barely sat down before she was back out of her seat, shouting, "He's gone! Kruger is gone!"

Her husband, Mike, walked in to check on her. "You're yelling like you just hit the lottery," Mike remarked. He was used to the roller coaster of emotions Karen rode with this campaign. Grief, anger, outrage, despair, frustration, hope. He was never sure what mood he would encounter, but he had not seen his wife this optimistic and happy since the retirees had celebrated stalling the Century bill at the statehouse.

"It's even better than that," she said, turning to look at him. "Logan Kruger is gone! He left Century!"

Karen could still clearly picture Logan Kruger's face, stone-cold and spiteful, as she addressed the board of directors. "It was like he was shooting daggers from his eyes," she would tell the retirees back in West Virginia. She left California convinced that Kruger was the embodiment of corporate America's ills—the greedy pursuit of self-interest and profit without regard for workers. She didn't hide her opinion of the man, either, referring to Kruger repeatedly as Century's "chief execution officer" in her written communication and in interviews with the press.

A retiree holds a sign listing Century's CEO's compensation.

Although she didn't want to admit it, and she didn't voice her concern to the others, she carried a worry that felt like an ulcer in her stomach: *We'll never change Logan Kruger's mind.* Now, they wouldn't have to.

The next day, Karen's phone rang repeatedly. West Virginia journalists covering the retirees' campaign wanted Karen's response to Kruger's departure. Karen shared exactly what she thought of Kruger, and her thoughts were printed, including her comparing Kruger to the Wicked Witch of the West. Karen followed the news about Kruger closely over the coming weeks. While Century's press release announced his resignation, Kruger had filed a lawsuit claiming breach of contract and wrongful termination, arguing he was pushed out of the company by the board of directors. According to an *American Metal Market* article, Kruger's severance package was substantially lower than the contractual severance Century previously had agreed to. *Well, what goes around, comes around,* Karen mused as she read the article. Still, she felt sick seeing the dollar amount. Kruger would receive $6.2 million in severance pay. This was $20 million less than if he left due to a change in control of the company, which he claimed had been the case.

Karen searched through the stacks of papers on her desk, remembering a profile of Logan Kruger she once printed. According to Forbes, Kruger's total compensation for 2009 alone was more than $4 million. The number was beyond comprehension. That someone could earn so much and still not be content, she couldn't understand. Karen told herself, *Every cent Mike and I have ever earned is just peanuts compared to what these CEOs make.* Which was true. If Mike brought home $40,000 a year (which could include working holidays and overtime) after thirty-three years, his *lifetime earnings* would have been $1.32 million—not even half of Kruger's compensation for one year.

In addition to following the news on Kruger, Karen had been watching news coverage of the Occupy protests that began in New York City in September 2011 and spread across the United States. The protests were the latest wave of mass movements emerging in the wake of the 2007–2008 global financial crisis. Organizers of the Occupy movement were calling attention to the effects of increasing economic inequality fueled by financial and political systems benefiting the top 1 percent of earners at the expense of the rest of society. Karen could appreciate this perspective and sympathize with the anger and frustration people were experiencing. She believed the Ravenswood retirees were victims of the ruthlessness and greed that she saw as driving decision-making in corporate America.

Felt acutely in communities like Ravenswood, uncertainty and instability had been undermining America's working class for decades. Industries that had thrived in the postwar decades of the twentieth century, particularly manufacturing, were declining. Workers bore the brunt of the impact, while US businesses might remain profitable for owners, even as production declined. As CEOs shifted their focus to maximizing financial gains for shareholders, decisions resulting in short-term profits had taken precedence over planning for the long-term viability of a company and the security of its workforce. At the same time, deregulation in the business and financial sectors increased the concentration of wealth among the wealthy, driving income inequality across the nation.

In 1965, when Kaiser ran the Ravenswood plant, CEOs on average earned 21 times what the average worker earned in a year. CEOs earned more than 60 times as much as the average worker in 1989, and 117 times as much by 1995. By 2009, CEO earnings had ballooned to 180 times an average worker's pay (and the gap has continued to widen). At the same time, companies publicly lamented the challenges of maintaining their obligations to retirees—carrying on as if workers themselves were to blame for living long enough to retire and expecting to do so with dignity and security. As Ellen E. Schultz documents in *Retirement Heist,* American companies raided workers' pension and retirement accounts to boost profits. At the same time, companies often built up lavish retirement packages for executives. Schultz agreed with companies' cries that America was facing a retirement crisis—but, she makes clear, it was no accident. Companies sacrificed their workers in order to benefit executives and shareholders.

Kruger's departure came almost three years after Century idled the Ravenswood plant, and despite her outrage over Kruger's claim for additional compensation, Karen had to believe that his leaving was good for the retirees. She

Occupy Century Aluminum camp. (Photo by James Fassinger.)

told journalist Jared Hunt that the lockout had ended after Ravenswood Aluminum Company fired several executives, and she was hopeful that parting with Kruger would signal a new chapter for Century. She shared this as rumors that Century was moving more seriously toward restarting the plant were gaining ground. In December, the *Charleston Gazette-Mail* published a story discussing the potential for a plant restart and quoted Karen as stressing that the retirees did not wish to be a roadblock but were determined to see the company fulfill its prior obligations—determined and willing to do whatever was necessary.

Occupied: December 2011–January 2012

Karen felt apprehensive walking into the union hall for the retiree meeting in mid-December 2011. She remained standing when she entered the back room, resting her hands on the back of one of the folding chairs. Conversations quieted, one after another, the retirees wondering if she might have some news about the restart. Karen always had some news to share. She was always talking to someone, always researching something, planning something. She looked a little nervous, though, fidgeting with the gold rings she wore.

"I know you all are going to think that I have lost my mind," she told the retirees, rolling her eyes when someone teased that they knew she had but loved her anyway. "Well, I have an idea," she said, sounding serious, "and I can't do it on my own."

"Tell us what to do, boss," someone replied, without a hint of hesitation.

"If you say no, I'll understand," she continued. "I know it's winter. But I say we get some tents and set up camp at the entrance to the plant, like the kids have done in New York and everywhere else. We should tell Century we aren't leaving until we get our health care. We should Occupy Century Aluminum." She held her breath for a moment, listening to the shuffling of bodies in chairs and the muffled sounds from the two offices near the front of the building. She wanted to give the retirees a moment to think about what she was asking of them.

"Karen, could we wait until after Christmas?" Hoot asked, breaking the silence. Luther "Hoot" Gibson was one of the oldest retirees fighting alongside Karen. He had hired on at the Ravenswood plant in 1958, after serving in the military. He started out sweeping floors and worked several jobs before training to be a millwright. He worked for almost forty years, half of those years on swing shifts, before retiring in 1996. Hoot and his wife, Lois, both active with the retirees' campaign, had been high school sweethearts. They married in 1955, and raised their two boys outside of Point Pleasant, West Virginia, south of Ravenswood. Their kids were grown now with kids of their own. Hoot had been looking forward to seeing them over the holidays.

"No, Hoot. We can't wait," Karen said firmly. "The legislature starts up in January, and Century will want to get that bill passed this year. We need to do it now." It was a big ask, she knew. At just shy of sixty-two years old, Karen was one of the youngest retirees committed to fighting Century. She took in the faces in the room, now questioning if she was crazy. Could she really ask these men and women to put their lives on hold, to miss Christmas, to sleep in tents during the coldest months of the year?

"I know this is—" Karen began, prepared to plead her case.

"OK, then. You heard her," Hoot said, looking around the room as he raised his hand. "Who's with me?" Two more hands went up, then three. Then more. Jim Weltner, Ripcord, John Morris, Les Shockey, and others were on board. Karen could feel tears welling up as she looked around the room. Before she could say anything more, the retirees were discussing the logistics of where to find tents and what supplies they would need to pull together.

Karen created a Facebook page for their protest that afternoon. She put out a call for donations, asking for firewood, inflatable mattresses, warm blankets, Christmas decorations, and prayers. In the next post, she shared that while Century's former CEO was handed $6 million once he was no longer of use to the company, West Virginia workers were left to die with no health insurance in their retirement. And still, $6 million wasn't enough for Kruger. "We are the 99%," she wrote, announcing that the retirees' Occupy Century Aluminum protest would begin on December 18, 2011.

Century Road branches from WV Route 2 a few miles south of Ravenswood. It branches again in about 250 feet, creating a Y shape to ease the traffic flow entering and exiting the

Century Aluminum and Constellium plants onto the two-lane highway. The retirees would transform this small triangle of earth contained by the two spurs of Century Road into their Occupy encampment. It was the same location they used for picketing, as it was visible to the Constellium employees coming and going from work and to the steady flow of traffic on Route 2.

On the morning of December 18, 2011, Bill Stephens hauled in a small, white, pull-behind camper. It wasn't new, but it was sturdy, and it would at least provide some refuge from the cold. If he and others were going to be spending nights here, they might as well be somewhat comfortable, he reasoned. Bill and his wife, Jean, were regulars at the retirees' meetings. Like a lot of men at the plant, Bill had hired on after serving in the army. He worked thirty-six years, retiring in 2007. He had worked with Ripcord and John Morris and Jim Weltner, and the others who were side by side with Karen, and he was glad to make this contribution to the camp.

Retirees surrounded Bill's camper with ten-by-ten pop-up tents reinforced with tarps. Two of the tents served as meeting rooms. A third functioned as a makeshift kitchen. Camping tents (most of them summer tents), for sleeping, littered the remainder of the space. The retirees raised an American flag at the north end of camp. A ten-foot wooden cross greeted drivers from the south. Dozens of handmade signs, run into the earth on wooden stakes, lined the camp's perimeter. The largest sign, declaring OCCUPY CENTURY ALUMINUM, stood at the north end of camp. In the middle of it all, metal barrels were converted into fire pits, where retirees would keep a fire burning during the long cold days and nights ahead of them.

Having trained in the art of picketing during the lockout, the retirees ran an efficient camp, signing up for shifts and sharing the work of hauling and splitting firewood. Two of the retirees' wives, Lois Gibson and Betty Jane Dixon, did most of the cooking for the group. They brought soups and chili and Crock-Pot meals on rotation. The camp also had a generator, and a propane camping stove, so folks could cook what they pleased. The retirees created a schedule for sleeping and picketing. Everyone had time at home and took turns for the overnight shifts. Some stayed for a few days at a time, covering their shifts, while others rarely left camp. Bill Stephens spent his days taking care of his farm and came out most evenings to spend the night. Ripcord, Hoot, and some others spent every day and night at the camp. Hoot left only twice a week to shower and change clothes. He had a large tent, a small portable propane heater, and a cot. Because of his dedication, the retirees voted him the official CEO of Occupy Century Aluminum. His wife, Lois, became known as "the chili lady" and was welcomed as an honored guest when she arrived with a Crock-Pot of food.

During the first week of Occupy Century Aluminum, Karen wrote on Facebook: "Corporate America can take our health care, but they can't take our heart and soul." She was feeling hopeful since they set up camp, inspired at how seemingly effortlessly it had come together, how invested the retirees were in running it, and how much support they had garnered from outsiders. Karen reached out to her media contacts, and it wasn't long before the camp made the papers, amplifying the retirees' message. "We will be here until we get what we paid for," Karen confidently told a reporter with the *Parkersburg News and Sentinel,* which ran a story on the Occupy camp a few days before Christmas.

It was a cold Christmas Eve but a festive day at camp. By late afternoon, when Karen's son, Chad Gorrell, and his wife and kids arrived, parked cars already stretched for a quarter mile down Route 2. Chad parked his truck and ushered his family up the road, keeping alert for passing cars. The Gorrell tradition, since Chad had moved out on his own, was that the whole family got together on Christmas Eve at Karen and Mike's house. But Karen knew she couldn't be at home, in a warm house, on a comfortable sofa, while others spent the day sitting on hard plastic and metal chairs under tarps. She had spent every day at camp since they set up and planned to be there every day until they had a deal with Century. Mike Gorrell also visited camp often and on Christmas Eve was there with Karen, along with dozens of retirees and family members and friends. They shared Christmas cookies and Crock-Pot chili, gathered around the fire or near the Christmas tree decorated with battery-powered lights. Visitors brought gifts of food, firewood, and extra blankets. Someone had opened a bottle of whiskey, and if it hadn't been for the weather, the camp could have been mistaken for a Fourth of July cookout rather than a protest. Karen welcomed Chad and his family with warm hugs and introduced them to what now felt like her second family, her "retiree army".

After the introductions, Karen bragged about her army the way one brags about those they love when they feel especially proud of something. She said that she had always known they were a special group but that this was extraordinary. She told herself that even if they had to go to the ends of the earth for their health care, she was convinced that they would find a way. They would have a good time doing it, too, she thought. Karen poured a cup of coffee from the camp kitchen coffee pot, laughing to herself. Recently, a retiree had discovered that with a long enough extension cord, the camp could "borrow" electricity from the plant by plugging into an outlet at the base of the illuminated Century Aluminum sign that stood on the opposite side of the road. They used it to run their coffee pots and a few other essentials and kept the generators on site to avoid suspicion.

After a couple of hours, Chad and his family said their goodbyes to their nana and the others and returned home. Mike Gorrell had gone home, too, and he called his son later that evening. It was Christmas Eve, and he was alone. He asked if Chad would mind stopping by the house. No problem, said Chad, imagining his dad busy with one project or another and needing an extra hand. Instead, Chad found his dad seated at the kitchen table.

"It's not supposed to be like this," Mike said, catching Chad off guard. The holidays, Christmas Eve, retirement. It was all a mess. It was all his fault, in this moment. His fault for working at that plant, for believing the promises. "This fight is killing your mom," he told Chad. More than anyone, Mike saw the effects that the stress of the campaign had on Karen's health, and he was worried.

On New Year's Day, the camp received news that Sonny Hinzman was hospitalized after a stroke. Sonny was one of the core group at camp and traveled with Karen and the others regularly for events. It was a solemn reminder for everyone of just how much was at stake. After the standard questions about his health, the retirees discussed whether Sonny could afford a lengthy hospital stay. He at least had Medicare coverage, the retirees knew, but he had not purchased any supplemental insurance for himself after Century ended his policy. He had opted to pay the premiums to continue with a COBRA (Consolidated Omnibus Budget Reconciliation Act) plan, but only for his wife and daughter, and that alone cost $1,700 a month.

Please, God, let us settle this before we lose anyone else, Karen prayed. She knew that with the recent media attention focused on the Occupy camp, any accidents or deaths would make headlines the next morning. Century knew this, too, Karen thought.

Retirees gathered at the Occupy camp.

The company had arranged to install a concrete median strip at the perimeter of the camp to separate the retirees from the traffic on Route 2. It was meant as protection from the possible car, or semitruck, careening off road in the snow and ice. It was appreciated. Karen couldn't help but clench her jaw and grip her sleeping bag when she heard the sound of a semitruck speeding past them on Route 2. But from the retirees' vantage point, Century was primarily protecting itself. If the company cared about its retirees' lives, well, they wouldn't be camped out here to begin with. Karen sat thinking about all this on one of those rare winter afternoons when the sun took center stage in a blue sky. *It's a sad state of affairs when bad press matters more than our lives,* she thought. In the end, though, she had to admit she would settle for knowing that Century was willing to do the right thing, regardless of its motivations.

Negotiations: January 2012–February 2012

On January 3, 2012, on the Occupy Century Aluminum Facebook page, Karen put out a prayer request for Sonny Hinzman, and announced that retirees would meet with United Steelworkers of America (USW) lawyers, and then with Century Aluminum, within a week. Less than one month after setting up camp, with the West Virginia legislative session looming, the retirees would have an audience with Century. If all went well, Karen let herself imagine, they could have an agreement for their insurance by the end of the month. They could have justice for Bryce and Sam. This could be over.

The meeting with Century was scheduled for January 10, 2012. The Retiree Committee—Karen, John Morris, Les Shockey, Jim Weltner, and Ripcord—drove from Ravenswood to Pittsburgh, Pennsylvania, to the USW international office. Century and the USW attended the meeting with their lawyers. The retirees were accompanied by John Beaver, president of the USW Local 9423 near Hawesville, Kentucky. John had worked at the Hawesville plant since he was twenty-one, hiring on in 1995. He had been the local president since 2010 and, in that role, had led the local's contract negotiations with Century. He knew how to read and negotiate a contract. He also understood the complexities of aluminum pricing and was generally good with numbers. More than that, the retirees trusted him. On their first trip to Hawesville, John Beaver spent hours with them, detailing all he knew about corporate accounting as it related to benefits and pensions, legacy costs, and liabilities.

When it sank in that the retirees were really going to sit down with Century and the USW to discuss a settlement, Karen had called John Beaver. As incredible as the news was, Karen had to admit, it was intimidating. She wished that John could go with them, she told him. John responded that he didn't see why he couldn't. He adjusted his schedule to get the days off, and made plans to travel to meet Karen and the others in Pittsburgh. If nothing else, he thought, Century would know that the Ravenswood retirees weren't fighting alone—that the union in Hawesville, which also had a reputation for being tough, was standing in solidarity with Ravenswood.

In the meeting, Century's lawyer made it clear that there was no going back to the previous insurance policies. Instead, Century would fund a voluntary employees' beneficiary association (VEBA) trust that would be managed by the USW. Retirees could be reimbursed with funds from the VEBA for qualifying health-related expenses such as insurance premiums. Karen listened to the lawyers talk back and forth and was reminded of the injunction hearing in Virginia. She was still upset with how that day had gone. The retirees questioned the VEBA, and when Century's lawyer said that the retirees could either accept it or take their chances in court, she snapped.

"I think you need to sit there and keep your mouth shut," Karen told him. "Anyone can go to court and lie and that's exactly what you did."

Karen left the meeting knowing there was work to do, but she felt confident that they were on their way. Of particular concern to retirees was the idea that the VEBA might not be funded until the Century plant was producing aluminum again. This would take time and wasn't guaranteed. "It needs to be better," was all Karen shared on Facebook after the meeting. The three parties would reconvene at a later date.

While they waited, the retirees celebrated the one-month anniversary of Occupy Century Aluminum, and in late January, the camp welcomed Governor Earl Ray Tomblin; the president and vice president of the USW, Leo Gerard and Tom Conway, respectively; Wes Holden, from Senator Jay Rockefeller's office;

and Kim Good, from Senator Joe Manchin's office. Their visits coincided with the ribbon-cutting ceremony for a new aluminum stretcher, a $46 million investment, at the Constellium plant. Several news organizations, the mayor of Ravenswood, and Jackson County elected officials all attended the ceremony, and those driving to Constellium from the north would have passed the Occupy Century Aluminum camp on their way to the event. It increased the retirees' visibility and publicity overnight.

By their seventh week, the day in and day out of the camp became the retirees' new normal. Yet even after living through the lockout, life in the camp was a test of their dedication. The cold chill in the air at night was the worst. It crept into their bones and made it hard to get moving in the mornings. Overall, though, they did well for their age. Their discomforts were balanced by the fact that they enjoyed each other's company immensely. Karen was beyond grateful to her compatriots. She loved her time at camp and felt privileged to be sitting with the retirees, listening to their stories, learning the nicknames and the practical jokes accumulated during decades of work. She valued their dedication to this effort but also their humor and lightheartedness, which helped keep her head from spinning when she worried about how much was at stake. "They are true American heroes," she would say in a Facebook post.

On February 7, 2012, Century Aluminum announced that Michael Bless was appointed the company's new president and CEO, having served in the role since Kruger's departure. Bless had been with Century since 2006 as their executive vice president and chief financial officer, averaging more than $1 million in annual compensation. Decades earlier, as a recent college graduate with a degree in medieval history, Bless began his career as an intern on Wall Street and then worked as an investment banker before moving across the table and climbing the corporate ladder. He had never intended to become CEO, however, and he was apprehensive when asked to take the reins after Kruger. He had always been a behind-the-scenes guy and had reservations about stepping into a public-facing role, navigating politics and relationships while managing the day-to-day operations of the company.

Despite these concerns, on his second day as CEO, Bless visited West Virginia and met with the retirees while on-site to tour the idled Ravenswood plant. Bless had been present for Karen's speech to Century's board in June 2011. He told her, later, that he remembered when the decision to terminate the Ravenswood retiree health plans came across his desk. He was the numbers guy. The numbers looked great. Terminating retiree health insurance would relieve the company of a major liability. He hadn't thought beyond that, he admitted, about the individuals who relied on this insurance, who believed they could rely on it for their lifetime.

Hearing that Bless was at the plant and planning to stop by the Occupy site, Karen hurriedly gathered everyone at camp together for a briefing, making it clear that the interaction needed to remain respectful. This was not the time for confrontation, she said. Bless was already showing the retirees more attention than Logan Kruger had in two years.

Bless parked the truck he was driving across the road from the camp. It was a shock to see the tents so close to the road. The speed limit here was fifty-five miles per hour. Terribly dangerous. John Hoerner, Century's North American vice president, and the Ravenswood plant manager were with Bless, and there was a crowd waiting, watching them exit the truck, with Karen at the front. Bless extended his hand to greet her, and Karen, before even introducing herself, assured him that everyone was friendly, which was more or less true, he found.

Then she hugged him. It shocked Bless, who hadn't grown up in a hugging family. Hadn't grown up in Appalachia. Hadn't grown up working class.

Despite having worked for six years at the company that had employed many of the individuals gathered now around him, Bless's life had not intersected with theirs directly before today. His world and their world, for the most part, did not overlap. The path open to Bless, early in his life, had included a reputable college and Wall Street. The men here had looked toward their futures and saw factories and mills and mines. At one time, these paths had held great promise. But those promises had been eroding for decades.

Bless told the retirees he was there to listen and that he hoped they could come to an agreement. He wanted to fix this, if he could. Karen said she hoped that under his leadership Century would show the retirees the respect they deserved. She talked at length about the hardships they faced and reminded Bless of those they had lost. She revealed the sleeve of her sweatshirt, printed with the words "Sam Matters."

"Sam McKinney should be alive today," she told Bless. "Before he died, Sam said that after he retired, it felt like his life no longer mattered to your company. Well, we are here to prove that it did matter. That every one of these people's lives matters," she said, looking at those around her. She was emotional as she spoke and blunt with her criticism, and Bless listened without interrupting. Unlike his predecessor, he seemed willing to give the retirees his attention.

That week, Century and the USW had a meeting scheduled without the retirees. Karen understood that the two parties wouldn't move forward with an official agreement but were hashing out some of the details. Then she answered a call from John Hoerner at Century. Hoerner had made repeated visits to Ravenswood since Kruger's departure in November

2011 and had met several retirees during their twice-weekly pickets at the plant.

"Karen, I couldn't wait. I had to know what you thought of the offer," Hoerner said.

"Excuse me?" Karen asked, caught off guard. "What offer?" Hoerner said Century was discussing a potential agreement, and Karen nearly dropped the phone. She got off the call to text someone at the USW, demanding to know what was on the table. Minutes felt like hours as she waited for the ping of her phone announcing a new email. She skimmed the first page of the document that had been sent. Funding for retiree health benefits would be contingent on the successful restart of the Ravenswood plant. Karen stopped reading.

"We don't have time to wait for the plant to restart," she said out loud to herself. She thought of Sonny, paying $1,700 a month for COBRA insurance and still not having any coverage for himself while recovering from a stroke. Medicare would only go so far, and he would have to pay what it wouldn't. She thought of Sam McKinney, too, and wondered how many others were choosing to go without the prescriptions they needed. Or how many, like herself, were forgoing any medical care. They couldn't wait a year or more for the plant to start up again.

After a restless night, Karen called one of the USW's lawyers.

"You lied to me," she yelled. "After the retirees got Century to the table! After the retirees have given everything to this fight." She hung up, slammed down her phone, and paced around her dining room table.

Karen spent the rest of the morning making phone calls—to the union and then to her contacts in DC and Charleston, including the governor's office. She followed up with Hoerner, telling him she had printed the offer and it now sat next to her toilet, where it belonged.

Karen was back at the Occupy camp in the afternoon, in a West Virginia University sweatshirt and camo jacket. She had done her makeup, hoping to hide her exhaustion. The phone calls had helped her feel less defeated, at least. She was able to voice her frustration and concerns, and she felt like she had been heard. Still, the last twenty-four hours had been trying.

She held back tears as she began to address the crowd. "I think we're going to do this," she said. "For the first time in a long time they finally understand where we stand and that we're dead serious on what they owe us." Sounding more confident, she added, "I talked to the governor's office this morning and they are 199 percent behind the retirees, and they are going to let Century know that they are behind the retirees." Though Karen had been hard on Governor Tomblin at first, it had been six months, and he had never wavered in his support for the retirees. More and more of the legislature had also come to support them. So Karen made clear that any badmouthing of the legislature or the governor on the part of retirees was to cease, immediately. Karen was careful not to compromise these relationships or to take the support for granted and wanted to be sure that anyone associated with the camp understood this. "These people are going to save our lives, and if you don't respect them, then get the hell out of here right now," she warned the crowd. Several retirees applauded and spoke their agreement.

"I'll take care of that problem," one of them said. Karen took a napkin that someone held out to her, wiping her nose as she continued. "I just want you all to know, and I don't think

I have to tell you, the retirees aren't quitting until we get the best that we can get."

"That's right," someone said. "Whatever it takes."

"And we're not going to be sold out by any damn body. We're going to get the best that we can get. You know I love you people, and I'll fight for you, and I'm going to do this until it gets done, but I told them today, damn it, I'm tired."

Chapter Seven

Catastrophic illness does not wait for PSC approval.
—Karen Gorrell

Deal: February 2012–March 2012

In mid-February, the Century Aluminum Retiree Committee (Karen, Jim Weltner, John Morris, Les Shockey, and Ripcord) prepared to attend a meeting with the United Steelworkers Union (USW) and Century in Charleston, West Virginia. Frustrated with the negotiations to date, Karen wanted to send a message that the retirees demanded being taken seriously. After talking through the details of the proposed settlement at length with John Beaver, the retirees feared it wouldn't go far enough. *We need a real offer. No peanuts,* Karen said to herself. Then she picked up her cell phone.

"John, we need to tell the world tomorrow that Momma K says, 'No peanuts for Century Aluminum retirees!' We need signs down there at camp. Can you get more poster board?"

John Morris grabbed his keys and left the Occupy site to make a trip to the Family Dollar in Ravenswood. Karen knew that the USW and Century and the West Virginia legislature were all anxious to clear this hurdle and to move forward with the legislation intended to entice Century to reopen the Ravenswood plant. But she wanted to do what she could to push Century toward an offer that would make a difference in the retirees' lives, and compensate them for the decades of contributions they had made toward retirement benefits.

Karen intended to make sure the retirees had a strong show of support during this meeting, and spent the day contacting supporters from West Virginia to the West Coast.

On the drive to Charleston, Hoot sat in the middle row of the minivan thinking about John Hoerner's recent visit to the Occupy camp. Hoerner had arrived with a bottle of bourbon—presumably a peace offering. Only Hoot and a few others were present at camp at the time. Most of the group had gone to an Alliance for Retired Americans Meeting in Ripley. Hoerner told the retirees about his father's tenure at an aluminum plant out West. He said the owners cut his dad's benefits, and his dad cursed them until his last breath. Hoot listened and let Hoerner do the talking.

In the van, Hoot turned to Les. "Hey, you remember when John Hoerner said his dad worked in an aluminum plant and lost his benefits?" he asked.

"I do. I still wonder if it was the truth," Les replied.

"Me too," said Hoot. "You know he gave me $40 before he left? Said it was so the whiskey didn't run dry."

"No, I didn't know that," said Les, shaking his head. "What did you do with it?"

"I put it in my wallet," said Hoot, with a laugh.

During the meeting, Hoot listened to Hoerner's company-speak, as he called it. The breakdown of the current and future financial challenges facing the company. The reasons Century offered to justify ending retiree benefits. When Hoerner finished, Hoot stood up and walked over to him.

"I've got something for you," he said, taking two twenties from his wallet, placing them on the table in front of Hoerner. "Sounds like you all need this more than we do."

After the meeting, Karen posted on Facebook, saying, "The support being given to the Century Retirees is just overwhelming and it reaches way beyond the boundaries of the Occupy Century Aluminum camp in Ravenswood West Virginia. Our support is growing nationwide and our voice continues to grow every day." Thanks to Karen's outreach, groups in Kentucky, California, and West Virginia held protests demanding a fair deal for the Ravenswood retirees. "Momma K says 'NO PEANUTS!'" their signs read. In Monterey, California, protesters left a large bag of peanuts with a note in front of Century's headquarters, sharing the photos with Karen and on Facebook.

The retirees, Century, and the USW planned to convene again at the end of the month with the goal of finalizing an agreement. "Keep the prayers coming," Karen wrote on Facebook, "that we will have a positive outcome that will benefit the retirees, the laid off workers, Jackson County, and the state of West Virginia." During the first day of these negotiations, journalists busied Karen's phone, hopeful for news, but there was little Karen could report. She shared on Facebook that "retirees are trying very hard to meet Century in the middle, but have not been able to come to a successful conclusion at this point."

Two days later, it made the news: Century and its retirees had an "agreement in principle" to restore retiree healthcare benefits. Governor Earl Ray Tomblin commended the announcement as a victory for the state. Senator Jay Rockefeller said he was "overjoyed." He and Senator Joe Manchin, in their official statements, credited Karen for her tireless and passionate commitment, and the USW for standing by its retirees. Karen shared her statement on the Occupy Century Aluminum Facebook page, writing, that "late this afternoon, with the help of the USW's Tom Conway, the unending support of Governor Earl Ray Tomblin and Senator Jay Rockefeller and many, many members of the West Virginia legislature, the retirees were able to come to an agreement with Century Aluminum for the restoration of benefits for the retirees." She went on to explain that the reinstatement of retiree benefits would be contingent on a successful restart of the Ravenswood plant, which depended on Century negotiating a new contract for electricity, and a labor contract with the USW. But all parties were now committed to moving forward. "The retirees are overwhelmed that the 'little people' could dance with the big boys and win the justice we were seeking," she wrote, noting that their experience could be a reminder to others to "never, ever give up, no matter how long the journey."

Of course, the journey wasn't over.

On March 1, 2012, retirees spent their final night at the Occupy Century Aluminum camp, after seventy-seven days, nearly the entire winter. That evening, the retirees ordered pizza, raised their plastic cups in a toast, and celebrated. They had done what they had come to do and were glad for that, though most would have stayed twice as long if they had needed to. Several retirees, including Ripcord, Hoot, Roy Daly, Larry Williams, and Sonny Hinzman (until he was hospitalized), had been at camp nearly every day, logging more hours there than at their homes. Karen, too, made the thirty-mile drive to camp every day that she wasn't otherwise occupied with events or travel. She kept herself busy, even as the negotiations were underway.

The next day, Hoot Gibson announced his retirement as Occupy Century Aluminum's CEO, claiming two bags of potatoes, camp-kitchen leftovers, as his severance. He spent his last day on the job with the others tearing down camp. Layers of tarps were peeled off the pop-up tents. Tent stakes were pulled up. Sleeping tents and sleeping bags stuffed back into bags and kitchen supplies packed into cars. Dozens of poster board signs that had been attached to wooden stakes were collected for burning. The American flag was carefully lowered and folded, and the ten-foot wooden cross was released from the earth that had held it. When the retirees finished their work, the only evidence of the last two and a half months were rectangles of bleached grass and muddied walking paths.

Despite the retirees' objection, retiree health insurance benefits would only be reinstated after a successful restart of the Ravenswood plant. This depended on Century and the USW agreeing on a new labor contract and the state legislature passing the Century bill, paving the legal road for lower electricity rates at the plant. The plant retirees, the hundreds of individuals represented in the USW's lawsuit, also needed to vote to officially accept the settlement.

The day before the retirees' vote, Senators Rockefeller and Manchin addressed the US Senate, praising the deal. Rockefeller commended Karen Gorrell for her dedicated effort, calling her "a local heroine" and "an icon of Appalachia." He stated that "this never could have happened without the leadership of Karen Gorrell, and her particular kind of leadership," saying she was the kind of person who could speak at a stockholders meeting wearing a "Retiree Blood Is on Their Hands" T-shirt and be respected rather than resented. He explained that while news of the settlement may not reach beyond West Virginia, it would certainly be big news in the state, as it was an example of labor and business coming together and rising to the occasion at hand. Both Rockefeller and Manchin also praised Mike Bless, USW president Leo Gerard, West Virginia governor Tomblin, and the West Virginia legislature.

Before the retiree vote, the Retiree Committee met with some of the individuals who would oversee the voluntary employees' beneficiary association (VEBA), wanting to review the relevant information one last time before they asked the retirees at large for their vote of confidence. As the Retiree Committee understood it, retirees over sixty-five could be eligible for a monthly stipend to cover costs associated with plan premiums and other health-related expenses. The younger retirees could be offered coverage through a new plan until they turned sixty-five. Now the committee learned that the specific details were still being sorted out. The retirees present for the vote would be given a document outlining insurance options and expense estimates for the retirees under sixty-five, but not a full description of benefits. Flustered, Karen called Raamie Barker, from Governor Tomblin's office. Raamie, like Wes Holden, had become a close ally for Karen. The advice and encouragement from both men had carried her through more than a few difficult days.

"Raamie, I'm supposed to ask these retirees to vote, and I don't even know what we're voting on. It's not what we thought we discussed." She knew they couldn't delay the vote. Retirees were already on their way to the high school.

"Karen, this is when you have to put your big girl pants on," Raamie told her. "You need to have that vote." If she had to sort out the details afterward, he told Karen, he would be there to support her.

In the Ravenswood High School gymnasium, Karen addressed over four hundred retirees who had gathered to accept or reject the proposed settlement that would offer them some reprieve after the loss of their health insurance. This offer was not the ideal that they hoped for, Karen told the crowd. It wasn't going to bring back the benefits that they had already paid for, and she couldn't tell them all the details at this time. But she knew Raamie was right. She told the crowd what they most likely already knew: that no matter what offer was on the table, it was more than what they had now. They had done without for long enough. They had sacrificed for long enough. Votes were cast on paper ballots and tallied that night. Karen called Raamie as soon as they finished counting.

"It's done," she shared. "The retirees accepted the deal."

Power: March 2012–October 2012

The morning following the retirees' vote, on March 16, 2012, Karen and a group of retirees drove to Charleston for the special legislative session where lawmakers would vote on House Bill 101, creating the Energy Intensive Industrial Consumers Revitalization Tax Credit Act. Walking onto a balcony looking down on the floor of the House, the retirees were greeted with a standing ovation. The room was jubilant, and as the retirees took in the faces of their legislators turned toward them, they felt proud and grateful. The applause seemed unending, punctuated by cheering, thumbs up, and waving from the thirty-one West Virginia lawmakers present who would vote to pass the Century bill, the first hurdle on the path to restoring retiree health care. Looking back on this day, West Virginia state delegate Mike Caputo told Karen that passing this bill, knowing the impact it would have on retirees' families, was one of the proudest moments in his long career with the legislature. Caputo spoke not only as an elected official but also as an international district vice president with the United Mine Workers of America—another union fighting to protect its retirees' benefits.

On April 2, 2012, Governor Tomblin sat behind a large wood desk staged inside Century Aluminum's facility in Ravenswood. Sandwiched between the state flag and a podium, he looked out on a crowd gathered to witness the bill's passage into law. Karen Gorrell sat in the front row and rose to stand behind the governor, joining the Ravenswood plant manager, the mayor of Ravenswood, and representatives from the USW and Century, to witness the moment the bill was signed. Afterward, sixteen Century retirees and their spouses shook hands with the governor and smiled for photos. The bill set the stage for Century to negotiate a labor contract and an electricity rate agreement for the plant, which now, finally, seemed destined to produce aluminum again. Newspapers predicted the plant could be operational in the fall, resulting in the return to Jackson County of between four hundred and five hundred jobs. Additional jobs could be expected in the years that followed.

In news coverage of the bill's signing, the Ravenswood mayor said that the plant restart would allow community members to start living their lives again. Statewide, unemployment had yet to recover from the recession, with thirty-three thousand fewer West Virginians employed than there had been at the recession's start. Employment in manufacturing jobs remained at a record low. Along with unemployment, drug use and related deaths had been rising since before the recession, and deaths from prescription opioids were now declared an epidemic by the Centers for Disease Control and Prevention. In Jackson County, the keystone of the economy had been compromised when Century idled operations, and the entire structure had been faltering ever since. But with the groundwork laid for the electricity tax credit, the Century plant was now one step closer to reopening.

Century and the Appalachian Power Company (APCo), a subsidiary of American Electric Power, needed to negotiate a rate agreement for the plant, and that agreement needed to then be approved by the state's Public Service Commission (PSC). Electricity accounts for around 40 percent of the cost of making aluminum, and Century spent a staggering $8 million a month on electricity when it idled the plant in 2009.

Securing a favorable rate for electricity was seen as essential to restarting the plant, and Century was proposing a flexible rate mechanism, reducing the amount the company would pay for electricity if the price per ton of aluminum dropped below $2,500. Century also proposed that the existing $17.3 million deficit it owed APCo be absorbed by other ratepayers, who had been paying on the debt since Century shut its doors.

Karen and the retirees followed the PSC negotiations as if their lives depended on the outcome—which, of course, they did. In June 2012, Karen sent a letter to the PSC on behalf of retirees, advocating for approval of the special rate structure proposed by Century. "Retirees' lives are tied to this decision," she wrote. Every month without health benefits was a month that she and hundreds of others would postpone seeing a doctor, not just for checkups, but also for acute and potentially fatal conditions. The retirees knew that they had done everything in their power to get Century to the negotiating table, and they were prepared to do everything they could to help move the PSC's decision forward. Unfortunately, the more Karen learned about Century's proposal, the more conflicted she felt supporting it.

Karen wasn't alone. APCo's attorneys remarked that the power company was very interested in seeing the plant reopen, but they had to consider, *At what cost?* The West Virginia Energy Users Group, representing the state's large industrial consumers, also spoke out against the proposal, arguing that Century shouldn't receive special favors. Some of these larger customers had been paying higher rates, up to 70 percent higher, since Century idled the Ravenswood plant. More than one hundred APCo customers also wrote to the PSC to express their disapproval of Century's plan. Century argued that these customers would be better off with the plant in operation, even with increased electric bills.

In July 2012, Karen and the retirees shared their concerns about Century's proposal directly with Century's new CEO, Mike Bless. In a second move that set him apart from his predecessor, Bless sat down with the retirees at a long table in the middle of the Cracker Barrel near Karen's home to discuss the issue.

"There has to be a better way," Karen told Bless. She had not expected him to be as sincere or as respectful as he appeared, she realized. She had certainly never imagined, after leaving Century's board meeting the previous summer, that she would one day sit down at a restaurant with Century's CEO. It intimidated her—the difference in their economic and social rank feeling more apparent the closer they were to one another. Karen had no professional background or experience in the matters they were discussing, but she took the fact that Bless was willing to hear her opinion to heart. She reminded Bless that the retirees had settled for less than what they had already paid for health benefits, that what they would receive in the settlement wouldn't add up to what they would have received with the contractual benefits Century had terminated. The retirees compromised in order to find common ground that benefited all parties, and now, it was Century's turn. After this meeting, Karen shared a statement with the press, writing that she had faith in Mike Bless to do what was right. She said she might be foolish, but she would hold out for "a fairy tale ending" where everyone wins, not just shareholders. "Century is certainly not the first, or only, company to terminate promised benefits to retirees," she wrote. "But I hope they will be the first to turn the trend in a different direction and honor their commitments of the past."

Following Mike Bless's meeting with retirees, Century submitted a revised proposal to the PSC, intending to address some of the first proposal's most controversial components, including the risks for APCo's other customers. As a result of the changes, Century could potentially pay up to $20 million more annually, and the company made clear that this was as much as it would compromise to restart the plant. Karen was impressed by Bless. Still, she thought of the retirees living on fixed incomes, already challenged by the loss of Century's health insurance. Under Century's rate proposal, these men and women could be asked to subsidize Century's electricity bills, while she knew there were retirees already struggling to afford to keep their lights on. Despite what was on the line, she couldn't advocate for retirees to receive money from Century for health insurance, only to pay higher electricity bills in return. Karen's position had always been that she was fighting for what was best for the retirees, who she believed had already sacrificed more than enough for Century.

On July 30, 2012, the PSC began a three-day hearing to review Century's special rate proposal, and Karen addressed the commission. "We want our state to bend over backwards to get that plant restarted," she said in her official testimony, "but not at the expense of the regular ratepayer." It wasn't the rate-payer's responsibility to provide retirees with their health care, and retirees wished their lives weren't tied to this decision. Speaking with Jared Hunt from the *Charleston Gazette-Mail*, Karen acknowledged that both Century and APCo needed to consider their shareholders, but she asked that they also consider Jackson County residents. In her heart, she believed that they would—that both sides had invested too much to walk away with nothing. "Let's get that plant open and let's join hands and let's stand together and watch that parking lot fill back up," she said, still hoping for her fairy tale ending.

Inspired by Karen and others' testimonies, Byron Harris, director of the PSC Consumer Advocate Division, created a "do no additional harm" plan that kept most of the components of Century's proposal but set a minimum rate to protect the company's other ratepayers. Harris argued that shifting the existing $17.3 million deficit Century owed APCo onto these ratepayers was unprecedented and already enough of a burden. Century's proposal was frankly, he said, "outrageous." He also argued that with the $40 million a year in incentives ($20 million from the state tax credits and $20 million from APCo via the rate proposal), Century should be able to operate its plant, if it were serious about doing so.

In early October 2012, the PSC announced its final plan. It approved a flexible rate agreement for electricity with a minimum rate to protect APCo customers but stipulated that Century could not walk away from the ten-year contract owing a deficit to APCo, even if Century no longer owned the Ravenswood facility. This agreement would provide Century the safety net it sought during times when aluminum prices were low, and it would protect APCo's ratepayers from having to foot a second bill from Century. The PSC noted that according to Century's own testimony, aluminum prices were expected to climb over the next ten years so that Century would not end the term with a deficit. In case the company's analysts were wrong, the PSC was simply seeking a guarantee of protection for West Virginians.

The following week, Century announced that the PSC's plan was not sufficient to warrant restarting the Ravenswood plant. A reporter from the *Charleston Daily Mail* called Karen a few days later. She had not prepared herself to accept that more than a year's work could be wiped away with one press release, that there might not be a fairy tale ending, after all. For Karen and those retirees who had devoted themselves to this fight, this news felt like losing their insurance all over again.

"We are sorry to say that even though we have faced many roadblocks along the way, that Century's recent decision felt

Century retirees' cemetery float in Hawesville, Kentucky.

like a knockout punch," Karen told the reporter. The retirees had put their faith in Century's new leadership, optimistic that Century and APCo would both be willing to make sacrifices to come to an agreement. Karen had trusted Bless. Now it seemed she had expected too much of him. She accepted this and agreed with those who told her, sometimes harshly, that she shouldn't be surprised that his loyalty was to his shareholders, not the retirees.

"They have dangled health care benefits and restoration of lost jobs in front of the retirees and the state like a piece of meat—just beyond our reach," she said, explaining that the state, the retirees, and so many others had worked tirelessly to extend a hand to Century. Maybe, she told the reporter, it was time for Century to sell the facility to someone who actually wanted to produce aluminum and to someone who could recognize a helping hand when it was offered.

You Decide: October 2012

Hawesville was once a small farming community in Kentucky, an hour and a half west of Louisville. Today in Hawesville, like in Ravenswood, a Century Aluminum plant sits a few miles from town on a gray expanse of concrete wedged between a state road and the Ohio River, among swaths of forest and farmland. Century Aluminum is one of several manufacturing businesses in Hancock County, which experienced significant industrial growth in the 1960s and 1970s and has remained a stronghold for American manufacturing into the twenty-first century.

Hawesville felt like a second home to Karen and the retirees. They felt welcomed by the local union like they were distant family, which wasn't far from the truth. Hawesville was a strong union, and like those in Ravenswood, workers here had endured an extended labor dispute, twenty-seven months, before Century took over ownership of the plant. At the last protest the Ravenswood retirees attended in Hawesville, Karen spoke with a worker after his shift, noticing he wore a large button pinned to his shirt. It read "Shame on Century Aluminum for Robbing Retirees of Their Health Care." He said a lot of workers wore them.

The USW local president John Beaver had taken the stance that the fight in Ravenswood was also Hawesville's fight, and his local voted each month to send the Ravenswood retirees a donation to support their organizing efforts. All this because John Beaver, and others, believed in what the Ravenswood retirees were fighting for and knew what was at stake. By now, it was common knowledge that Century was looking for a more favorable power deal for the Hawesville plant. If they didn't get it, Hawesville might go the same route as Ravenswood.

In October 2012, the Hawesville plant hosted a Health, Wellness, and Safety Fair for workers and their families, with vendors, activities, and lunch provided. Retirees were welcome to volunteer, a flyer for the event announced.

"Well, I suppose that means we're welcome," said Karen facetiously, sharing the flyer with the Ravenswood retirees at one of their meetings. She suggested that the group travel to picket at the event. Now that Century had backed out of the power deal with APCo, Karen was focusing on elevating their platform outside of West Virginia, where she worried they were losing ground. Plus, the retirees were aware that Century was taking a proactive approach to PR in Hawesville, showcasing itself as a company that cared. Earlier in the year, Century announced in a press release it had raised $90,000 in a fundraiser to aid a Hawesville employee battling cancer. Meanwhile, Karen said, all the company had offered Ravenswood so far were empty promises.

"They think if they can keep up their image in Kentucky, no one will remember the grandmas and grandpas dying without health care in West Virginia," Karen said as they discussed the details of the trip to Hawesville. "But we're not going to let anyone forget."

Karen, Les Shockey, Jim Weltner, John and Mary Morris, and others drove to Hawesville the night before the company health fair. They made their way down winding back roads to the home of a Hawesville retiree, Pete Shouse, who would loan them a flatbed utility trailer to use as part of their protest. The retirees had plans for constructing a float, of sorts. Covering the bed of the trailer with square hay bales, they positioned more than a dozen white wooden crosses and cutouts of tombstones among the hay. Each grave marker and cross had the name of a retiree who had passed away since Century first terminated their health insurance plans almost two years earlier. Bryce Turner, Sam McKinney, W. L. "Willey" Henry, Alden M. Deal, Coy Wade, Clarence G. Barker, and others were memorialized.

The next morning Pete Shouse delivered the retirees' cemetery trailer to the road next to the Hawesville plant entrance. Across the road, with the sign for the Hawesville plant visible in the background, retirees set up their second prop, borrowed from the AFL-CIO (American Federation of Labor and Congress of Industrial Organizations) office in Charleston, West Virginia. The fourteen-foot-tall inflatable "Fat Cat"—a giant cartoonish cat, red with yellow eyes and fangs, stood upright, dressed in a blue suit and gray vest, one hand gripping the neck of an inflatable "worker"—a Lego-looking character wearing a hard hat. The retirees hung a handwritten sign around the cat's neck: "While retirees fill the graveyards, Century 'Fat Cats' fill their pockets!!"

Three retirees were staged at the plant's entrance with the mock cemetery and Fat Cat. They talked with those who stopped their cars and held signs for the cars that kept driving. The rest of the group drove on to the edge of the plant parking lot, where they set up their own "information booth" just beyond the official event. On a trifold poster board, the retirees stapled copies of their benefits termination letters next to the health fair flyer, which stated, "Century Aluminum Cares about the Health and Safety of Our Employees, Retirees, and Families." They came with handbills presenting the two documents side by side. "LIES?? YOU DECIDE" was printed across the top of the page.

Throughout the day, Karen and others made their rounds through the crowd, passing out the handbills and talking with employees. The union employees in attendance were kind and receptive, already having a strong relationship with Karen and her army, but Karen could sense that their presence was also making some people uneasy. At one point, Karen spoke with one of the salaried employees she recognized. She had been standing back from the event for several minutes, listening to the music and watching the workers and their spouses eating, talking, and laughing. She would have enjoyed this event in Ravenswood, she knew, before everything went south.

"Eric, this breaks my heart," she confessed to the employee. "I know the plant manager spent a lot of effort putting this together, trying to show Century's good side. It's a good event. It's a beautiful day. People should be enjoying themselves." She wiped tears from the corner of her eyes. She had always worn her emotions on her sleeve, and there was no sense trying to hide it. "But Century is the only one who can fix this. All they have to do is what they promised: take care of their retirees, and we won't come back." She paused a moment before making her own promise. "Until then, even if I hate doing it, I'll be here."

Karen had an internalized set of rules that governed her campaign, and this event fell at the edge of her comfort zone. She would picket any day and happily inconvenience or embarrass Century's management team by calling out how they had treated the retirees, but she had no interest in antagonizing workers. She and her companions were always civil and well mannered, and today was no different; however, she had gotten some looks. They had reminded her of the lockout and the way people looked at one another with either suspicion or contempt, the way families and neighbors and friends were divided, and the tension that had seemed to have an unrelenting grip on the town. If her involvement with the lockout had inspired her current "take this as far as we can" approach, it had also inspired her to consider restraint.

Karen had often reflected on some of the uglier memories she had of the lockout. She thought of the time when she came home to find her children, Chad and Jodi, then twelve and seven, respectively, trying to fasten pencils together to make jack rocks—two nails welded together and used to flatten car tires. Or when she got into a screaming match at the Parkersburg Mall while shopping with her son. That was the first time she heard Chad use a curse word. She was disappointed that she had dragged him into that fight. It had been important to Karen that her children understand the union's value and the hard-fought benefits that unions had won for workers. She wanted her children to know the power of standing up for their rights and to understand how being part of a union meant being part of a family that always supported one another. She wanted her children to be proud of her father's legacy. She also knew that while the lockout had brought out the best in their union, it brought out the fight in everyone, and she could look back and say that there were moments that she wasn't proud of.

Then again, the retirees were much older than they had been during the lockout. Too old for jack rocks, perhaps. And it was true that none of her army would have thought to make any trouble. Karen repeatedly emphasized the fact that these were honest, hardworking, "play by the rules" retirees. Her repeated message to those who showed up for any picketing or events was that they were to be *respectful*. It was why she had told anyone who wanted to criticize the West Virginia legislature to get the hell out of their Occupy camp and why she had insisted that the camp be solely for retirees, after young people from other cities and states had tried to join them. Karen had seen the conflicts between Occupy protesters and the police play out on the news and didn't want to take any chances that someone would get out of line. She knew that negative press was used to discredit the Occupy protesters as vagrants or troublemakers. She knew that from the lockout as well. Karen took into consideration that the retirees in this fight were the underdogs who held the moral high ground, and that was what mattered to her the most. She worked hard to never compromise that position.

Chapter Eight

As we watch the actions of Patriot Coal, we are reminded of the extremes corporate America will go to in order to rid themselves of their promised and paid for obligations and their legacy costs. It is time that the American people get some back bone and stand up against what we consider criminal behavior.

—KAREN GORRELL

Respect: November 2012–September 2013

By November 2012, Century had submitted two alternative proposals to the Public Service Commission (PSC) for consideration: one plan for an immediate restart of the Ravenswood plant and a second that could be pursued when aluminum prices were higher. Neither plan included the protections for ratepayers the PSC had demanded, and in December 2012, the PSC denied Century's request. The changes proposed by Century warranted a new proceeding, it determined. It also advised Century to pursue negotiations with the Appalachian Power Company (APCo) directly rather than ask the commission to mediate a deal.

In those final months of 2012, Century repeatedly stressed its commitment to a Ravenswood restart. But by early 2013, Century's negotiations for electricity rates in Kentucky—then the top aluminum producing state in the US—were overshadowing the company's efforts in West Virginia. After months of negotiations with the Big Rivers Electric Corporation in Henderson, Kentucky, Century gave notice that it would terminate its contract with the utility in August 2013. Following

Century retirees and supporters with the "Fat Cat" in Chicago.

this news, a second aluminum smelter, in Sebree, Kentucky, announced it would also terminate its electricity contract with Big Rivers the following year. Together, the loss of these two contracts could result in rate hikes as high as 30 percent for the remaining Big Rivers customers.

Following their West Virginia playbook, Century looked to Kentucky's lawmakers for support. Two bills were in the works that would allow large industrial consumers to purchase electricity on the open market rather than from local utility companies. Unlike West Virginia's, the Kentucky legislature declared these decisions should be made between the utility providers and individual companies, concerned about the precedent set by asking the state to intercede. However, with the future of two large employers and more than one thousand jobs on the line, there were also concerns about the precedent Century had set in West Virginia—closing its doors and laying off its workforce. By March 2013, the governor of Kentucky was urging all parties to come to an agreement.

Meanwhile, more than a year had passed since the Ravenswood retirees walked away from their Occupy camp toward the promise of a plant restart and renewed insurance benefits. Now they seemed no closer to that end than when they first set up their camp the previous December. Even with four months until the settlement agreement would expire, Karen was told it was unlikely Century and APCo could reach a rate agreement and secure PSC approval by that deadline. Karen worked hard to find enough hope within herself to inspire the others. If she gave up now, it would be the end of the line for everyone, she told herself. Instead, the retirees would have to ramp up their campaign. They discussed opportunities for new events, including a twenty-four-hour protest at the entrance to the Ravenswood plant.

On March 7, 2013, Jim Weltner hauled in a recreation of the traveling cemetery they constructed in Hawesville to their former Occupy site in Ravenswood. The retirees set up tents and signs, and again made a makeshift camp that would house them, this time just for one night. They proclaimed to visitors, including local news reporters, that America's senior citizens had suffered enough abuse at the hands of corporations, and it was time that someone did something about it. If that had to be the retirees themselves, so be it. Karen made clear that while they were losing faith in Century's new leadership, they weren't giving up on a settlement and were still very much committed to their cause.

In late April 2013, Century announced the company would close its Hawesville plant in August, laying off 750 workers, if it couldn't reach a rate agreement for electricity. Less than two weeks later, the company reached a tentative agreement with Big Rivers and Kenergy Corp. for market-based electricity rates and announced the $61 million purchase of the Rio Tinto Alcan aluminum smelter in Sebree, Kentucky. Now not only did Century have the electricity deal it wanted, but it was acquiring a newer smelter. Mike Bless stressed that the purchase would not impact the company's plans in West Virginia, however. The Ravenswood restart was still a priority.

Until it wasn't. On July 1, 2013, the agreement reached by the retirees, the United Steelworkers (USW), and Century regarding retiree health benefits officially expired. On the same day, the final group of Ravenswood retirees (those laid off when the plant was idled in 2009, who then applied for early retirement) lost their company health insurance benefits. In an earnings call in late July, Century announced that other priorities had taken the place of restarting Ravenswood and that the company would need a competitive power deal, like the one being negotiated in Kentucky, to move forward.

Karen did her best to stay optimistic despite the disappointment that ached like heartburn. She didn't want to admit, even to herself, that the last year had taken a toll on her health—mentally and physically. But there was no option except to keep fighting. She made this commitment again and again, as friends and family asked, cautiously, what she planned to do now that the settlement deal had expired. She told them all that she had made a promise to Bryce Turner on his deathbed, and she planned to keep her word. She wasn't giving up until the retirees had their insurance or she took her last breath.

During the month of August 2013, the Ravenswood retirees returned to Kentucky to protest Century's acquisition of the Sebree facility, held another two-day protest at the Ravenswood plant entrance, and made several visits to Charleston to connect with their state representatives. They had come too far and gotten too close to give up. It was getting harder, though.

Some retirees were spending a significant portion of their pensions to cover health expenses and had been doing so now for two or three years, depending on their age. Jim Weltner paid over $650 a month just on his premiums. He had retired with a good pension, $1,500 a month, but the medical costs ate into it, including the twelve prescription medications his wife took daily.

"I hope they put our name on the title at Sebree," Karen wrote to the retirees. "Because that's our money they spent to purchase it." Jared Hunt, for the *Charleston Gazette-Mail*, wrote that Century reported quarterly savings of up to $18 million from terminating West Virginia retirees' health insurance benefits. Without that savings, the retirees argued that the Sebree purchase would not have happened. Karen wrote to Mike Bless to tell him what she thought about the Sebree purchase and made the same promise to him she had made at the Hawesville Health Fair: until this was settled, the retirees weren't going away.

On the morning of Century's annual shareholders' meeting in September 2013, ten Ravenswood retirees arrived early, preparing to protest and address the board of directors for a second time. Earlier that year, Century had relocated its headquarters from California to Chicago, receiving $700,000 in tax credits. Mike Bless had pushed for a move to the Midwest when he became CEO, wanting management to be closer to Century's facilities and customers. As a result, the company's headquarters was now within driving distance of Ravenswood.

This meeting would take place at the hotel connected to the O'Hare airport. Before the meeting, Mike Bless met with retirees in the hotel hallway. Karen, Jim

Weltner, Larry Williams, Hoot, John Morris, Ripcord, and others stood around Bless in a half circle. They wore blue jeans and their now iconic bright blue shirts with bright red handprints, with the text "Century Aluminum Robbing Retirees of Life-Sustaining Contractually Promised Healthcare! Our Blood Is on Their Hands."

Bless, wearing a dark suit and blue tie, sneezed and wiped his nose as he explained to the retirees that the company was working out how to move forward with APCo. "You guys think it's all words, and that's fine," he said, sounding either sick or tired and perhaps unconvinced that he could change their minds. Still, he offered, "I don't know why we would still be trying like this if we weren't sincere. It would be a ridiculous waste of time." The retirees stood attentively, watching Bless as Karen reminded him that the retirees had always treated him with dignity and respect. More than he deserved, she said, given how Century had treated them.

"They offered their handshake to you, and they told you, all we want is what we paid for. How hard is that?" she asked.

Hoot stepped up, gently placing a hand on Karen's shoulder, asking if he might say something. He spoke calmly, with a slow drawl, explaining to Bless that Century told him they were canceling his health care because it was necessary to restart the Ravenswood plant. "You took that money, and what did you do with it?" he asked Bless, calmly. "You didn't restart Ravenswood. You took my money, and you bought another plant in Kentucky." He looked down at Bless through his large square-framed glasses. "And you want me to believe everything you say?" He crossed his arms in front of his body, waiting for Bless's response.

"I understand that's how you look at it," Bless said, quietly.

"What other way is there to look at it?" asked Hoot.

Karen reminded Bless that it had been six months since she last heard from him and that each day that this dragged on was agonizing for the retirees.

"I may have had a stroke a week ago," she said, holding back tears. "My grandkids were there, and they watched me, and they begged me to go to the emergency room. I wouldn't go because I don't have any health care." Bless lowered his gaze, like a child admitting that he broke something valuable. "You don't understand that, do you, Mike?" she asked. "You can't understand because you live in some high place," she said, "but we live in the real world, Mike, and we need this settled."

As they continued, Bless's voice and demeanor became quieter. Karen reminded him that Century had turned its back not only on retirees but on the West Virginia statehouse, which had put in substantial effort on behalf of his company. She let him know what the retirees thought of Century's lawyer, too, who had acknowledged to the retirees that they were owed benefits but was now arguing the exact opposite in court.

"That's what lawyers do," was all Bless could offer, insisting that he was still doing everything he could to move forward on their behalf.

"But are you going to make this happen, or is it a pipe dream?" Karen's tone and her look demanded an answer.

"It's not a pipe dream," Bless told her, as another man in a dark suit and blue tie walked up to Bless, presumably to let him know it was time to leave. "This is Terence Wilkinson," Bless said to the retirees, as Wilkinson extended his hand to Karen and those standing close by. Bless explained that Mr. Wilkinson had been added to the board of directors as chair the year prior.

"Then you know why we're here," Karen said, turning to him, not ready to end the conversation.

"Yes," Wilkinson responded, assertive and agreeable, like a politician. "And we respect your position." He added, "I just want to tell you, too, that a more genuine and straightforward person on the subject than Mike you won't reach."

"Well, you can ask these guys," Karen said, motioning to the retirees, "I've always said that there is something different about Mike Bless. I believe that," she said, but she added that what hurt her the most was that she had to conclude that the retirees' lives didn't actually matter to anyone at the company. Otherwise, there was no excuse to drag this ordeal out for years. "We've sat down to dinner with this man," Karen said, looking at Bless.

John Morris stepped forward, addressing Wilkinson. "I hope Mike can be the guy you say he is," he said, sincere, before asking Wilkinson if it made any sense to him that the retirees would have contributed so much of their pay toward benefits if they thought they would expire. "How long do you believe your retirement benefits are going to last?" he asked, quiet but firm. Wilkinson didn't answer the question but asked to make a statement, as if speaking on record, perhaps acknowledging James Fassinger's cell phone recording him. Fassinger, a photographer and journalist from Detroit, had met the Ravenswood retirees while covering the Occupy movement and had traveled to meet them in Chicago for the shareholders' meeting.

"I am pleased that I've had the opportunity to meet up with you," Wilkinson said. "Remember the words I've used: I respect you." He looked around at the retirees. "I sincerely do," he added, matter-of-factly, as he turned and walked away.

Karen addressed Century's board of directors later that morning as she had done two years before in California. She made the same case, presenting the same argument: the retirees of this company deserved the same dignity, respect, and consideration as any one of the men staring back at her. These retirees had families and were part of a community that was built around the Ravenswood plant. They had paid their dues at that plant and did so with the promise of retirement benefits. Century had no right to go back on this agreement, and the company should be ashamed that it had left some of America's most vulnerable citizens without the ability to see a doctor or pay for prescription drugs. It should be ashamed to steal from these men and their families—men who, by now, after three years of the retirees' campaign, the management at Century should know by name.

It was a long drive that evening through Indiana and Ohio. Karen was quieter than usual. At some point, John Morris remarked he couldn't get over how thin people were in the city. He thought it must be all the walking they do downtown. That, and the price of a burger was twice what it cost back home. He laughed. Karen wanted to laugh but only managed a smile. Her thoughts continued to drift to Mr. Wilkinson. *He respected them*, even after all the hell the retirees had raised. They had embarrassed the company's former board chair publicly, and they called Century's executives murderers. They had recently crashed a company event in Hawesville, and they put the brakes on a state tax credit worth millions. But Karen knew she did her best to lead with integrity. She had never called anyone a name they hadn't earned, and she never had to doubt that she was on the right side of this fight. Wilkinson's words had an effect on her, she couldn't deny that. But she also reminded herself his respect didn't mean much, given Century's track record. Real respect was given in actions, not words.

Larry Williams stands for a photo on Century Road.

Faith: October 2013

Sebree is a small northwestern Kentucky town sitting to the west of a wide bend of the Green River, thirty minutes south of Evansville, Indiana. It was founded as a rail town in the 1860s, swelling to a population of 1,500 by 1910. The population receded to under 1,000 by 1930 and would not record any large gains until the 1980 census, when it again topped 1,500. In 1970, the Anaconda Aluminum Company had announced it would invest $100 million in a new aluminum plant in Sebree. Anaconda employed 375 people when the plant began production in 1973, and though the plant remained productive, Anaconda's tenure was short-lived. Alcan acquired the smelter in 1985 and then Century in 2013.

The Ravenswood retirees were incensed over Century's purchase. While some retirees had only worked for Century for a fraction of their careers, they had been loyal to the Ravenswood plant regardless of who wrote their paychecks. Century's loyalties, they believed, were unreliable—shifting to align with whatever deal could benefit the company most. Workers. Retirees. Unions. All of them were expendable. So as a courtesy to their fellow workers, in early October 2013, the Ravenswood retirees decided to let Sebree know exactly what kind of employer Century had proven to be in West Virginia.

"This might be worse weather than Cleveland," Jim Weltner said from the driver's seat, keeping his eyes on the road. Jim did a lot of the driving when "the army" traveled long distances. He enjoyed it, most of the time. Today, though, the trip was seven hours through steady rain. They were nearing their destination and accepting that they were going to spend the day under umbrellas until, minutes outside of Sebree, the sun brightened the sky.

"I think God just might come through for us today," Karen told the group, eyeing the clouds as Jim parked their van. She wanted that to be true. Needed it to be true. The last year had been a test of her faith and her resolve.

The retirees set up their picket on the road leading to the Sebree plant parking lot. Traffic was steady during shift change, and the retirees took turns speaking to Sebree workers in their cars as they exited the plant. The set up looked like the roadside fundraising drives held by small-town volunteer fire departments, with the addition of signs and banners calling attention to the retirees' cause. Their picket routine was a well-oiled machine by now. Today, as Karen predicted, even the weather cooperated. The sky was gray, but early October leaves offered a show of color. There wasn't a drop of rain.

Karen noticed Larry Williams had been standing next to the same car for ten or fifteen minutes. She moved closer out of curiosity and could hear a woman telling Larry she would pray for the retirees and their victory.

"I know the Lord is going to help you win," the woman said. Karen joined Larry, and the two of them spent several more minutes talking to a woman who must have been close to retirement age herself, they guessed. She seemed in no rush to end the conversation, and they realized they weren't either. The woman's faith was refreshing to them both.

"That woman today, she had a way about her, didn't she?" Larry asked Karen that evening, as dusk settled around them and they loaded back into the vans. Karen agreed. She wished she had asked the woman's name.

The following week, Karen picked up a package at the retirees' box at the post office in Ravenswood. Then she sat with it in her car, unsure what to do. She called her husband.

"Don't open it," Mike advised. Karen eyed the package in the passenger seat the way a hiker eyes a copperhead sunning itself on the trail. It was the size of a large book and addressed to "Century Aluminum Retirees." There was no return address. "I'm just saying, you've upset a lot of people," he told her. "And there are some crazy people out there."

Since the settlement deal expired, Mike had been more direct with his doubts about Karen's decision to keep up the campaign. For three years, she had worked tirelessly, but the deal had fallen through. It wasn't her fault, but he didn't see what else could be done now. For more than a year, Karen's family had quietly worried that this fight might be her last. The toll it was taking on her health was becoming more apparent. Karen was unafraid to speak her truth, and Mike worried when he read some of her more opinionated quotes in newspapers. He feared that one day she might upset the wrong person. An unexpected, unmarked package just made him uncomfortable.

Mike was only stating out loud what had already gone through Karen's mind. Maybe someone did want to shut her up, she thought. Still, she had to trust her gut, and something told her that this was OK. So she hung up with Mike, talked to God, and opened one end of the package. Carefully. She tipped the box and let the contents fall into her hand: a Bible, and a handwritten note: "Give this to the man with the cane at the end of the road." The sender included a list of selected passages to read for encouragement, the note explained. Karen sighed and held the book to her chest, tears dampening her eyes.

Larry and his cane, Karen said to herself, starting her car and smiling now, picturing Larry Williams, braced on his cane talking to that sweet older woman in her car in Sebree. Larry Williams was in his seventies. Looked like he could be a Kenny Rogers impersonator, he was told, though he had a bad knee now and relied on his cane to get around. Larry was usually one of the first to volunteer for Karen's plans. He was there for the rallies, pickets, and protests, and his smile and sense of humor helped some of the darker days feel lighthearted.

At the next retiree meeting, Karen presented Larry with the Bible. It was a welcomed lifting of spirits in what was otherwise a low-spirited meeting. They were doing everything they could think of, and it seemed like none of it could make anyone at Century give a damn about their lives. Karen had barely contacted anyone at the union since the deal evaporated, she told the retirees. It felt to her like they were on their own now more than ever. But that wasn't exactly true, she decided that evening, as she looked through letters and photos and newspaper articles that she had collected over the years. She had three scrapbooks put together, and a box of mementos and documents yet to be filed. She kept every card she had received. Several were displayed on her desk, along with a note from Sherry Breeden at the AFL-CIO (American Federation of Labor and Congress of Industrial Organizations), quoting Margaret Mead: "Never doubt that a small group of thoughtful, committed citizens can change the world; indeed, it's the only thing that ever has."

Looking over these artifacts, Karen considered that while the settlement, their one big win, had turned into their biggest letdown, there were these small moments that felt like victories. Like the Bible for Larry, and the miracle of keeping Bryce Turner insured until the end of his life. There were the open arms that welcomed them wherever they went. The checks that came in the mail from other unions, like the USW local in Hawesville, the United Mine Workers of America (UMWA), and the Communication Workers of America. There were phone calls and emails from the retirees' allies and supporters, offering advice or just a kind word. Karen had even had Senator Rockefeller and Wes Holden at her house for dinner, on Rockefeller's invitation. *What do you cook for a*

US senator? she had asked herself, feeling panicked initially. Roast beef, she decided, with potatoes, carrots, and onions and apple pie for dessert. He went back for seconds, she would say proudly when she shared the story. When the settlement deal was announced, Wes had arrived at the Occupy site with flowers for Karen from the senator, congratulating her on her efforts. The accompanying card, which now sat on her desk, was addressed to the "Hero of Appalachia."

The last three years had led Karen down a path that would have been unimaginable the day she began her campaign. She was angry as hell a lot of the time, and her stress levels were unhealthy. She had been completely devastated and heartbroken more than once, but she felt honored when thinking of the generosity and support the retirees had received. It was as unexpected as it was remarkable, often coming from total strangers. Of course, kindness wouldn't get the retirees' health care back, but Karen was convinced that it had to add up to something. At her core, and in spite of the challenges and the relapses into doubt, Karen believed that God would see them through this. She also knew that although not everyone shared her beliefs, faith was part of the bond that held her "army" together. Bill Stephens, who shared Karen's strong faith, served as the unofficial chaplain for their group. He opened events and meals with prayer, and at their biweekly meetings, he regularly opened with a prayer for retirees who were ill or undergoing surgery.

Karen's own faith and her promise to Bryce were what kept her from walking away from the campaign after the settlement deal expired. She knew and was reminded often that the retirees did not walk their path alone; there were greater forces carrying them forward. Somehow, in a way that Karen couldn't quite put in words, receiving this Bible felt like a sign she had been waiting for.

Century retirees march with the United Mine Workers of America.

Covered: October 2013–December 2014

Seven years before losing Century's health insurance, Karen had lost 116 pounds, which she credited to her involvement in a Taking Off Pounds Sensibly (TOPS) group in Parkersburg, West Virginia. Her two grandchildren were toddlers at the time, and Karen wanted to be there for them. Healthy, for them. But by November 2013, she had been so consumed by the campaign for retirees that she was ready to give up the TOPS meetings. She had already given up the three-mile walks she took religiously, three days a week, and she was gaining back the weight she had lost. She was also smoking more—chain-smoking, and sitting for hours a day in front of the computer, or on the phone, trying to make some progress. Even when working at the bank, she had moved more than this. The other women in her TOPS group had witnessed the change in Karen since she became involved with the retirees' fight—the stress and the effects it had on her health. So they saw to it that Karen didn't stop coming to their meetings. They made her "pinky promise," a joke among the women, because if you made Karen pinky promise, they said, you could be sure she would never break her word.

Karen left a TOPS meeting in Parkersburg one winter evening and stood brushing a dusting of snow off her car in the parking lot. As she reached across the windshield, she felt a sharp stabbing pain in her back and winced. She walked back inside the building and leaned against a wall to steady her breathing. Her friends rushed to her side, frightened. She was pale. They pleaded with her to go to the emergency room, well aware that she had been having heart palpitations. Karen refused. Just thinking about going to the hospital without insurance raised her blood pressure. After resting for a while, she felt OK to drive herself home. Karen had not visited a doctor since her COBRA (Consolidated Omnibus Budget Reconciliation Act) coverage ended in the summer of 2011—more than two years before. When the deal was reached with Century in 2012, she reasoned that she could take care of her health once Century was paying for their insurance. Now, although Century remained "committed to finding a solution" to a plant restart in Ravenswood (according to a recent news article), the retirees could see little to show for that commitment. The prospects of Century paying for insurance seemed to be diminishing, and those close to Karen were beginning to voice the concerns about her health and well-being that they had been keeping to themselves.

When the Affordable Care Act (ACA) enrollment period opened in October 2013, Karen looked into purchasing a plan through the new health insurance marketplace. The ACA offered tax credits to offset the costs of premiums, but Karen was disappointed in her options. The annual deductible was around $7,000 and monthly premiums were still higher than she and Mike could reasonably budget. It was catastrophic coverage, at best. She decided to pass, reasoning that she would be eligible for Medicare in a year. Plus, she wasn't keen on letting Century off the hook. Karen had to wonder if corporations weren't counting on the ACA to address their *early retiree problem*. Going forward, early retirees facing the loss of their company insurance would have a safety net in the ACA marketplace plans. Even though the plans weren't ideal, Karen considered that they might be just enough to keep retirees from getting up in arms about the loss of benefits from their employers.

Wes Holden, with Senator Rockefeller's office, knew that Karen was worried about her heart. He was also worried. In the years since the Ravenswood retirees had lost their insurance, Wes had supported individual retirees by connecting them with services and resources, helping them navigate their most immediate health-care needs. After the incident at her TOPS meeting, Wes advised Karen to look into a clinic that provided services on a sliding scale, targeting those above the threshold for Medicaid but still considered low income. Karen didn't qualify, she learned, but Wes was concerned enough to call in a favor to get her checked out. Since she wasn't technically eligible for their services, the clinic wouldn't be able to provide any follow-up care. But Karen could at least be seen and know the prognosis.

Karen sat with her husband in the parking lot outside of the clinic, wishing she could cancel the appointment. It was the first time in her life that she had relied on any kind of formal assistance program. She felt heavy with guilt for knowing she was technically *too well off*. She fidgeted with her rings, a nervous habit, and then decided maybe she shouldn't wear them inside. Did she look like a fraud, she wondered? It was just a onetime visit, Mike reminded her. He understood her reservations. They both knew, without discussing it, that this was hard on Mike too. He had never had to ask for help and had worked long and hard days and nights so that his family would have everything they needed in life. But he absolutely wanted Karen to see a doctor.

Karen had not worried this much about her health in a long time. Not since the lockout, now that she thought about it. She had gone to the emergency room back then—her first and last time—and still remembered the doctor sitting close to her, asking if she had been under any unusual stress. She thought of this as she walked back to the car where Mike was waiting for her. The doctors had done several tests to check Karen's heart and would follow up with the results. They were letting her go home, though, and that at least was a relief. In addition to the concerns with her heart, she still didn't know what had caused the episode that had made her lose her vision temporarily—what she thought could have been a stroke—but it hadn't happened again. She was not driving for now, just to be safe.

On the drive home, Wes called Karen to check in. He had more news to share.

"Karen, I'm not supposed to tell you this, but I made another phone call—" Wes paused before adding, "—to Mike Bless. I told him you were having problems and that it might be your heart. I said if anything was wrong, Century should be the one to pay for it since they're the reason you're in this mess." Karen knew that Wes was frustrated that retirees remained without benefits. He also knew more than most how much effort Karen was putting into this fight. Like Karen, he believed that

Century could have fixed this situation if that was their goal. "And Karen, Mike agreed with me. So don't worry. Whatever you need, we'll find a way. It will be covered."

"What do you mean, covered?" Karen asked, hopeful, thinking of insurance.

"You just focus on taking care of yourself." Wes had been venting his frustration when he called Bless, and Bless sympathized. He spoke not as Century's CEO but as someone who knew Karen and who, like Wes, hoped to offer her some peace of mind.

Karen held her breath for an instant and held the phone away from her face, trying not to cry. She hadn't fully realized how worried she had been about the worst-case scenario: blocked arteries, open-heart surgery, and the bills that would follow. She couldn't believe she was hearing this now. Nor could she accept it. She took a moment to gather herself before responding.

"Wes, you know how much I appreciate you, and how grateful I am. But, I'm sorry. Nobody is going to cover anything," she said defiantly.

"Karen—" he began.

But she continued. "Until Century wants to cover health care for all the retirees, I'm not going to accept any kind of favors, from anyone. I have to be able to live with myself, Wes. And I'm not the only one suffering because of this." Karen thanked Wes for everything he had done. He was a true friend. Hanging up the phone, she and Mike sat in silence for several long moments. She felt him keeping his eyes on the road ahead, knowing he wanted to say something. She waited.

"Karen, this is your health," he finally told her. "No one is better off if you let this kill you." The two of them didn't talk much about the fight with Century anymore. When they did, it was the same conversation. They were both stubborn. Mike told Karen that she had done her best but that it was time to move on. One person could only do so much. Karen understood his concerns and regretted that she had dragged him and the rest of the family into this, but that was a regret that she had to live with.

"There's nothing in me that could bring me to accept an offer that isn't going to help the retirees," she told her husband. After a pause, knowing what Mike was thinking, she added: "I can't walk away from this either. I made a promise to a man on his deathbed, Mike. I'm not giving up." Karen would be eligible for Medicare in less than a year, she reminded him. She could make it until then, she promised. Then she would get back to seeing a doctor.

Karen still hoped that the Ravenswood retirees might be some of the last to go through the ordeal of losing health insurance and having nowhere to turn. Karen held out hope that there could be federal legislation passed. She and the retirees had continued to meet regularly with their state and federal representatives to discuss the issue. They were also encouraged to see that the UMWA was making headlines for pushing back against Patriot Coal after a judge's ruling that the company could cut union-negotiated benefits as part of its strategy to emerge from bankruptcy. The UMWA and others claimed Patriot Coal was designed to fail: the company was never meant to be profitable. Instead, it was a way for Peabody Coal (and later, Arch Coal) to break its promises to workers and walk away from the responsibility of lifetime benefits. Critics pointed out that when Patriot Coal was spun off from Peabody in 2007, it acquired 13 percent of Peabody's coal reserves and 40 percent of its health-care liabilities (the benefits owed to workers and retirees). By 2012, the year Patriot filed for bankruptcy, the company was responsible for pension and health-care obligations for twenty-two thousand retired miners and spouses. Most of these retirees had never actually worked for Patriot, having retired before the spin-off. Like the Ravenswood retirees, however, these miners had worked for decades with the understanding that they would receive lifetime benefits.

The maneuvering out of benefits obligations was not an altogether uncommon move for US companies. However, Peabody's approach of offloading these liabilities through a spin-off company was considered particularly bold. Patriot and Peabody denied the accusations, and Patriot claimed several factors contributed to its financial problems, not just the burden of liabilities. Still, whatever hardships the company faced, executives did just fine. The year before filing for bankruptcy, Patriot Coal CEO Richard Whiting (who worked as an executive at Peabody Coal before joining Patriot) received $4.3 million in compensation.

"Shame on Patriot!" Karen wrote on Facebook after a group of Ravenswood retirees joined the UMWA at a march in April 2013. "We know first-hand what it feels like and the devastation created when corporate greed tries to destroy the retirees that worked decades to build their corporation!" Thousands turned out for the march, and Karen was inspired by the energy and enthusiasm that the UMWA's leadership brought to the campaign. They were successfully drawing national attention to their cause.

A year later, in June 2014, US senators Jay Rockefeller and Elizabeth Warren (D-MA), with cosponsors including Senator Joe Manchin, introduced the Bankruptcy Fairness and Employee Benefits Protection Act in the US Senate. The bill would limit companies' ability to terminate worker and retiree benefits during bankruptcy. It would also establish the presumption that benefits cannot be cut after a worker retires and would require companies to provide clear language outlining the duration of retirement benefits. These latter provisions, Karen believed, could have protected the Ravenswood retirees, who lost their benefits outside of a bankruptcy. With this bill, there might be hope for others.

By early September 2014, Century's stocks had doubled in price from just four months earlier, and Mike Bless announced that he hoped to be able to share a more substantial update on Ravenswood by the end of the year. The company was reporting "reasonable progress" in its discussions for a power deal with APCo and still considered the Ravenswood plant a top priority. Before any update on Ravenswood was announced, however, Century announced the purchase of an aluminum facility in Mount Holly, South Carolina, for $67.5 million. Cash. (Century already had nearly 50 percent ownership interest in the plant.) Taken with the Sebree purchase, Century had invested over $120 million in acquisitions since walking away from the PSC's offer in West Virginia. This was more than the company estimated it would have needed to invest in Ravenswood to restart the plant.

Karen had heard rumors that Century would assume the obligations for benefits for retirees at their new Kentucky and South Carolina facilities, and she vented her anger on the phone with Paul Nyden, a reporter for the *Charleston Gazette-Mail*. She claimed that she would have expected these decisions from Logan Kruger, certainly, but not Mike Bless. "I will soon be 65, and I am still uninsured," she told Nyden. "That makes me furious. Today's news adds salt to our wounds."

Chapter Nine

Having meetings every two or three months that result in more questions than answers is not my idea of progress.
—Karen Gorrell

Progress: January 2015–June 2015

By January 2015, the Bankruptcy Fairness and Employee Benefits Protection Act had died in committee, never receiving a vote. The rate agreement between Century and the Appalachian Power Company (APCo) for the Ravenswood plant seemed destined to die out as well. Senator Jay Rockefeller and Wes Holden both were retiring, leaving a void in Karen's network of supporters. Acknowledging that they could have a long year ahead of them, the retirees continued to commit to their biweekly meetings, and to considering all possible paths open to them.

For three years, the Retiree Committee had spent hours discussing how to offer retirees a fair deal while remaining within the parameters set by the 2012 settlement agreement. The committee had expanded by now to include Hoot Gibson and Mel Lawrence, along with the original five members: Karen, John Morris, Ripcord, Les Shockey, and Jim Weltner. Mel, being one of the under sixty-five retirees who showed a dedicated interest in the retirees' organizing efforts, was asked to join to represent the interests of the younger retirees. Hoot was then officially voted in to keep an odd number of members. He had been sitting in on the committee meetings since 2012.

An ongoing point of frustration among the original committee members was that the oldest retirees, who had contributed more of their pay toward retirement benefits during their careers at the plant, would receive less of a payout from the settlement than the youngest retirees, who would presumably spend more years collecting reimbursements from the voluntary employees' beneficiary association (VEBA). The wage concessions that employees made to fund these benefits over thirty or forty years added up, and that should count for something now, they reasoned.

In a February 2015 letter to Mike Bless and Century's board of directors, the Retiree Committee laid out its request for a just settlement. It used $44 million, taken from the 2012 negotiations, as its starting point, reminding Century that this was less than the company's original contractual obligation for benefits. It was also less than the $60 million purchase of the Sebree, Kentucky, facility, the $60 million Mount Holly acquisition, or the $60 million spent in recent years on stock purchases. The committee assumed receiving more than $44 million from Century was unlikely, and its members saw only one option for equitable compensation that would not raise that price tag—they were asking for a lump sum payment.

"This requirement is not negotiable," they wrote. The committee had met with multiple VEBA account administrators and insurance adjusters to discuss the issue and had determined that a VEBA was "not in any way in the best interest of retirees." Instead, the committee proposed that the $44 million be allocated to retirees based on years of service, in a one-time payout. They believed this arrangement would reflect the actual value of wage concessions made by each retiree during their tenure at the plant. The longer someone had worked and paid for retirement benefits, the more money they would collect from the settlement.

The committee reminded Century of the support network the retirees had established throughout West Virginia—a network "that absolutely agrees that our request is reasonable," the committee wrote. Committee members also noted that the retirees were still an important asset in the ongoing negotiations with APCo and in securing the eventual vote of the Public Service Commission (PSC), saying, "We are confident the probability for positive outcomes improves dramatically if we move forward as assets and not adversaries." After sending the committee's letter to Century, Karen forwarded it to Governor Tomblin, West Virginia representative Mitch Carmichael, US senator Manchin, and United Steelworkers (USW) international vice president Tom Conway, asking each of them to support the retirees' request for a lump sum payment. Karen received positive responses in return.

In the spring of 2015, Century was caught up in negotiations for a new power contract in South Carolina, while disagreements over a new labor contract in Hawesville, Kentucky, were escalating tensions with the local union. Both events took time and attention away from Ravenswood, Karen knew. It felt like she had been holding her breath for weeks, waiting for news, when on April 30, 2015, Jared Hunt reported for the *Charleston Gazette-Mail* that Century might walk away from Ravenswood. He quoted Bless as stating that the company couldn't afford to keep the plant idled indefinitely. Either APCo and Century would finalize an agreement soon, or Century would, unfortunately, have to cut its losses. Weeks later, the *Gazette* ran an article outlining APCo's response to Century—the company was not holding up negotiations but was unable to agree to Century's proposal because other ratepayers would be affected, and this required PSC approval.

Disappointed, and feeling helpless, Karen wrote to Bless directly, letting him know that she was losing faith in his promises. She had nothing else to lose, she reasoned, by sharing her frustrations and accusations with him directly. "I am made to look like a fool for believing in Century's words," she wrote. Karen also shared precisely what she thought about the situation in Hawesville, now that Century had announced its intention to lock out 570 Hawesville workers. "What in the world are you thinking?" she asked. "Do you and the board of directors sincerely believe that walking away from negotiations by locking out the Hawesville employees is doing anything to improve your current position?" Century had brought in "replacement workers" to train at the Hawesville plant *during* the contract negotiations. These out-of-town workers were ready to take over the reins the moment the Hawesville workforce was out the door so that the company could maintain production should the union strike. Predictably, Century's actions soured morale at the Hawesville plant, turning workers against the company.

In her email, characteristically long and as impassioned as a preacher's sermon, Karen told Bless that Century promised economic security—steady, good-paying jobs—but "only if the elected officials and the workforce and the community caved to your demands . . . to ensure that you could succeed." She wrote that treating the workers in Hawesville with respect and dignity should be a given. "Or is common sense not a part of corporate America's reality?" she asked. She added that sooner or later, playing the "corporate bully" was going to catch up to Century and signed her email:

> Proud of who I am,
> Karen Gorrell

In Bless's response to Karen, he reminded her that workers had now voted on four different contract agreements that Century was told would pass a vote. The final modified contract offer, intended to prevent the lockout, was voted down by 60 percent of workers on May 11, 2015. Karen reminded Bless that Hawesville workers were paying higher electricity costs at home to subsidize Century's new power deal in Kentucky—workers who could soon be prevented from entering the plant. She explained that these workers were being forced into overtime shifts, a remaining point of contention in the contract, and they were worn out. The least Century could do was listen to them. She encouraged Bless to show up and hear what workers had to say.

"I think YOU could make a difference," she wrote. "You have proven your willingness to hear from the opposition. This is your company right now, Mike. Please . . . make the trip." The lockout would be hard on Hawesville workers and families, Karen knew. She also knew a prolonged labor dispute wasn't going to do Century any good. When she heard that Bless was open to talk to the union in Hawesville, she reached out to assure Hawesville union leadership that there was still room to negotiate with Century. Don't give up yet, she told them. She agreed with her contact in Hawesville that things could be better. The contract could be better, and Century could continue to negotiate in good faith. She knew this was true, but she also knew from experience that things could be much worse. If she could take any action that could help steer Hawesville away from a prolonged lockout, she would, without hesitation. This wasn't her fight, some told her, but Hawesville had treated Karen and the Ravenswood retirees like family. They were her union family. In a matter of days she had inserted herself as a mediator, advocating for both sides to listen to one another. Primarily, she insisted that Bless try to understand the workers' perspective.

When Bless mentioned the reported threats of violence from Hawesville's workforce, Karen wrote at length about how she had known "bad apples" from the Ravenswood union, but these individuals were not in the majority. She had learned that anyone, even those you would never expect to step out of line, could be pushed to their edge when their livelihood was at risk. Bless needed to understand what was at stake for workers, and she asked him to consider that when productivity and profits increased at the plant, it was because of workers. Yet the shareholders were the ones to see the benefits. She mentioned the stories told by the Ravenswood retirees of working under Henry Kaiser, who greeted workers in the Ravenswood plant by name when he visited. Most of Century's top management and the board of directors had never stepped foot in Hawesville, she assumed. Or Ravenswood. They were out of touch, and Karen needed Bless to see that. A little respect would go a long way, she was convinced.

"I truly believe that if you and the local could have some dialogue even once a quarter, only great things will happen in Hawesville," she told him. "They see that operation as 'their' plant the same as you see it as 'yours.' The only way everyone wins is if both sides have a common goal." Karen explained to Bless what she understood to be the primary issues for the Hawesville workforce. Forced overtime was a major point of contention, but the company was also trying to scale back benefits for new hires. "What it comes down to is respect," Karen wrote. "Have you or Hoerner ever spent sixteen hours on top of a hot pot—do you have any idea what that's like? And you think you can tell these men to do this, and then tell them they don't deserve benefits?" Karen reminded Bless, as kindly as she could, that he had no idea what this job entailed or how physically difficult the work could be. He probably had not spent sixteen hours in his entire career inside a potroom. All he understood was corporate's point of view. "You need to get on a plane and sit down with the negotiating committee and hear what they have to say, Mike," Karen insisted. If he wanted to understand what was really going on in Hawesville, he had to go to Hawesville.

Century and the USW were already working with the Federal Mediation and Conciliation Service to facilitate negotiations, and Bless did travel to Kentucky, meeting with the union in Frankfort, the state capital. Soon, the two sides had agreed on a new labor contract that the workforce approved, ending the lockout after just one month. In an email, Bless thanked Karen for the role that she played and for encouraging him to get involved—it was the push that he needed, he said. He also acknowledged that the end of the lockout had put out the biggest flames in the fires that had kept Century's management preoccupied. With this situation settled, attention could be focused on securing power deals in West Virginia and South Carolina. "Now," Bless wrote, "on to Ravenswood!"

On to Ravenswood!: June 2015–July 2015

The end of the Hawesville lockout reenergized Karen and boosted her confidence in Century—or, at least, in Mike Bless. In her last email on the subject, Karen told Bless it could signal "a new beginning" for the relationship between Century and its labor force, and invited Bless to join her in traveling to Hawesville to celebrate. "I am so happy! Happier than I have felt in several years!" she wrote. It wasn't an exaggeration. It had been two years since the agreement between Century and the Ravenswood retirees had expired, and Karen admittedly had very few reasons to be optimistic since then. She needed this victory to remind her that victories were still possible.

Turning her attention back to Ravenswood, with new enthusiasm, she focused on mediating discussions between

Century and APCo, believing that she could help the two sides move closer toward common ground. She and the retirees met with Senator Manchin's office to solicit the senator's support, and she kept Bless informed of the steps she was taking. She then wrote a three-page letter to APCo's CEO Charles Patton, explaining the plight of Ravenswood retirees and their stake in the Century-APCo agreement. She counseled Mr. Patton to consider the broader impacts of the power arrangement and his role in finding a way forward. "Are we going to be part of the problem or part of the solution?" she asked. "Are we going to work hard to find a plan that works, or are we going to watch the Ravenswood plant be dozed into dust just as we watched Ormet meet its sad and devastating demise?" Ormet had operated an aluminum smelter in Monroe County, Ohio, and had cited the Public Utilities Commission of Ohio's decision not to approve the company's proposed "energy transition plan" as justification for closing the facility.

> I am asking you and Mike Bless to step back from the business aspect of this situation and take a closer look at the human factor. Our communities need these jobs. Our state needs these jobs. And our country needs these jobs that pay a living wage and can take away the hopelessness so many young families are living with today. These kinds of jobs are NOT easy to come by or readily available in our state. We have a drug problem that is ravaging our communities and taking many lives. A restart of Century would provide several hundred good-paying jobs and many more secondary jobs. The boost to Jackson County would be immeasurable, as it's beginning to look like a ghost town.

Karen also reminded Patton that while the retirees had little left to sacrifice at their age, they had been more than willing to compromise at every turn to reach a solution that was good for everyone, including APCo and its ratepayers. "It's the right thing to do," she said, "and at the end of the day, that's all that matters." Karen told Patton that his company's current approach to negotiations with Century was not working. She challenged him to sit down with Mike Bless because she believed the two of them would determine the outcome of this situation. She would challenge Bless to do the same.

Afterward, she was glad to have said her piece. It was a good letter. She sat at her computer, debating her next move. She had talked herself out of emailing Bless for the last few days, not sure if she should share what had been weighing on her mind. Bless was a busy man. It astonished her that he responded to her emails. She knew he could always choose not to, and she didn't want to push her luck. But rumors were circulating that Century was pulling the plug on Ravenswood for good. Some said they heard it from John Hoerner himself: June was the end of the line.

She wanted to believe the talk wasn't true, she wrote, when she couldn't hold off any longer on sending the email. She thought forwarding Bless her letter to Mr. Patton was a good pretense for reaching out. She was keeping him informed. She also told him that she needed an honest answer, and Bless counseled Karen not to listen to the rumor mills. Century would not have committed the time and expense involved in these negotiations just to walk away.

In June 2015, APCo offered a new proposal that would allow Century to purchase power on the open market. Century responded that market rates were higher in West Virginia than in Kentucky and the offer wouldn't go far enough. They would lose money, Bless said. Century again proposed offsetting a reduced electricity rate for Century by increasing other customers' rates—a plan that nearly no one besides Century supported. Karen was becoming more anxious. Neither side seemed to be making any honest concessions, and she encouraged Bless to offer the state some confidence that a deal would result in a restart of the Ravenswood plant as soon as possible. She let him know that the current circumstances were distressingly similar to those two years ago, when Century walked away from a deal that the statehouse, the union, the federal government, and the retirees had spent considerable time and energy working to come to an agreement on. From her perspective, Century had not repaired the trust that was damaged.

Karen's eyes were on the road ahead of her as she made her way through a green light at an intersection near Mineral Wells, West Virginia. She didn't see the other car coming from her right. The other driver didn't see the red light. She closed her eyes, tight, and tensed her body at the moment of impact, as soon as it had registered that her car was no longer in her control. The sound of screeching brakes and crunching plastic echoed in Karen's head after the collision. Her heart pounded. Her car was in bad shape but not totaled. Karen was bruised and badly shaken, but nothing appeared to be broken. She agreed to go to the emergency room. She had turned sixty-five this year, finally, and enrolled in Medicare. She wondered, though, if this had happened a year ago, would she have refused to see a doctor? Probably, she thought, and felt her anger. It needed little encouragement to surface with the adrenaline from the car crash flowing through her. She tried to calm herself, mindful of her racing heart.

The doctors reported there was no significant damage from the accident. However, they discovered a lump on one of her adrenal glands. Additional testing showed no cause for concern, and as relieved as she was by the news, she also realized she felt a little guilty. So many people she knew were facing new health challenges. Les Shockey's wife was battling cancer and blood clots in her lungs. Peach, as he was known, who had been active with the retirees' efforts since the beginning of their fight, was facing his second round of cancer. Karen feared he was at the end of his days. Peach was someone who could make the group laugh when no one felt like laughing. Karen thought about him daily, prayed for him devotedly, and missed his company dearly. There had been dozens of funerals for retirees in the last five years, and she worried there could be dozens more before this was settled, given how discussions were progressing with APCo and Century. Karen had recently talked to another retiree who decided to forgo prescribed heart medication after open-heart surgery because his Medicare drug plan wouldn't cover the cost. The prescription would have raised his monthly health expenses to over $1,000, while his pension was only $600 per month. Even with Social Security, it just didn't add up. Karen thought of Sam McKinney, and how this same calculation likely cost him his life. She thanked God every day that since Sam McKinney had passed, she had not had to say goodbye to anyone in the small group of retirees who stood by her side day in and day out. But she knew that wouldn't be true forever.

"If you find the time, please update me as to where you stand with Ravenswood and any progress or lack thereof," Karen wrote to Bless in June 2015, at the end of a long email discussing the details of Karen's ongoing research and effort to further the APCo negotiations. She was concerned about an article she had read about the poor outlook for aluminum production in the US. It was another pretense to reach out. She hated to keep pressing the issue, hated to feel so uncertain and to think that the retirees were at the mercy of markets and the men who obeyed or controlled them. She didn't know which, anymore. She just knew she needed someone to give her a clear answer and decided on a simple question: "Did we survive the board meeting?" So far, there had been no official word on the subject of Ravenswood, but there was no power agreement yet either. Karen pleaded with Bless to be up front with her. Weeks passed, and Karen checked her email multiple times a day, before writing to him again.

"No news doesn't feel like good news," she said. She was desolate. The spark of enthusiasm ignited after the end of the Hawesville lockout had burned to ash, and she didn't understand why, but it seemed like the negotiations between Century and APCo had stalled entirely, and she wasn't getting any straight answers. Bless responded in time, saying that he would like to meet with Karen and the Retiree Committee. It was important to him that Karen be there, he said, and they agreed to meet after Karen's daughter's wedding, scheduled for the following week in South Carolina.

Karen and Mike Gorrell had taken the family on vacations to Myrtle Beach since their children, Chad and Jodi, were young. As an adult, Jodi continued the tradition with her son, Jackson. This year, Jodi's entire family, Jodi's fiancé's family, and close friends of the couple would come together for the week for her wedding ceremony. The highlight of their time together would be the exchanging of vows on the beach, surrounded by loved ones. Seeing her daughter happy made Karen happy. Jodi deserved this. And Karen needed this break, she admitted. Short of being hospitalized, being there for her children or grandchildren were the only reasons she would have postponed a meeting with Mike Bless. Thankfully, her family had been healthy these last several years. Their lives were more or less settled. Chad had the one scare, back in 2012, when back problems had led to emergency surgery. For weeks, he was unable to walk. In those first days after his surgery, Karen had camped out in his hospital room in Charleston, more than an hour away from her home. She drove back and forth to her house to shower and change clothes, and spent that entire time on her phone, catching up on the retiree effort. Besides this, there had been no major events, and she had been granted a leave of absence from her regular nana duties. It had only been a few years, but Chad's kids didn't need to be dropped off at their grandparent's home after school any more. Karen knew it was because they were old enough to take care of themselves, but it was shocking how quickly that had happened. Soon enough, the grandkids would be driving and then moving out to start their own lives.

Back in West Virginia, still caught up in the magic of the wedding, that much-needed infusion of joy and merriment into her life, Karen wrote to Bless to confirm details for their meeting. She felt hopeful, she told him, but she wasn't holding her breath. Neither were the other retirees, who had less faith in Bless than Karen did, though they were thoughtful to not be discouraging. On Monday, July 25, 2015, the Retiree Committee drove to Charleston and sat down with Mike Bless at the office of Tom Heywood, one of the lawyers working for Century on the PSC negotiations. Karen had always liked Heywood. She trusted him, as she had come to trust Mike Bless. Bless told the retirees that he had news he wanted to share with them personally before it was made public. He was holding the press release until he could sit down with them face to face.

"We've done everything we could. We aren't going to be able to restart the plant," Bless said, explaining that the board had made its decision. The retirees stood as if stunned for a moment. Each of them was used to bad news by now: a phone call announcing another friend or former coworker had passed away, a doctor uncovering a new chronic condition to be managed, a loved one's health scare. These were potholes in the road that they learned to navigate around, and of course, they were accustomed to bad news from Century. But it didn't make this any easier. Eventually the retirees turned to Karen, who looked like she'd just been given a terminal diagnosis. She felt like it too. The joy that she had carried home like a cherished memento from the wedding was shattered.

"That doesn't mean you can walk away from us," Karen told Bless, meeting his eye, holding back tears. He could plan to see her in September at the next annual shareholders' meeting, she promised.

Aluminum's End: July 2015–December 2015

On July 28, 2015, West Virginia newspapers announced Century's closure. It was a disappointment for all parties who had invested considerable time and effort in negotiations with the company. Still, Karen affirmed her commitment to continue her efforts, despite being "broken-hearted." This was not the end of the road for retirees, Karen made clear in interviews with the journalists asking for her opinion on the closure. And she wasn't alone. In their press releases, elected officials from DC and West Virginia lamented Century's decision. West Virginia governor Tomblin and US senators Rockefeller and Manchin made statements asserting that Century still had a debt to settle. Manchin wrote, "Although I am saddened to hear of the permanent closure, I will not stop fighting to bring these jobs back to West Virginia, while also ensuring Century keeps its promise to retirees." West Virginia delegate Mike Caputo echoed this position, writing, "We must do all that we can to see that these retirees are fairly compensated, and the promise of health care is upheld."

The only positive that could be spun from Century's decision was that the end of uncertainty, as disheartening as it was, was welcomed. The *Charleston Gazette-Mail* quoted the mayor of Ravenswood, Mike Ihle, saying that the town had already suffered the worst impact of this loss, as it had now been six years since the plant employed a sizable number of people. Ravenswood had reported strong business growth in the previous year, and the town remained an ideal location for new businesses, the mayor asserted. Marking a small step forward, Constellium Rolled Products (located beside the Century plant) soon announced that it expected to hire nearly twenty additional workers in the years ahead. It was a far cry from the 650 jobs that Century cut in 2009, but it was something.

When Bless shared news about the plant closure with them, the retirees had left with the impression that this decision did not close the door on retiree health care. It couldn't, officially, with the court case still pending. The retirees' fate had yet to be decided, and though the faith the retirees had in the court case had eroded over time, it was something they could hold on to, for now. So Karen emailed the USW lawyer representing the retirees' case. She requested a meeting, saying that new discussions were in order now that Century had made their move and left the plant to rust. The Retiree Committee had information it believed could make a difference in their case, Karen wrote. "We had several bullets we refrained from using because we did not want to jeopardize the restart of the plant. But if that possibility is gone, and if Century's board does not come through, we plan to fire every bullet we have." Karen informed the lawyer that if he were unable to meet with the retirees, she would share the information they had gathered directly with the judge, in an open letter, which she would also pass on to West Virginia state representatives.

The retirees had committed to attending Century's shareholders' meeting in September 2015, but Karen put off booking her hotel room, finding it difficult to convince herself that the trip would be worth the expense of time and energy. The disappointments of the retirees' campaign were weighing on her the way depression weighs on a person. It clouded everything in her life. Even the good moments, like Jodi's wedding, were experienced as if a part of her were somewhere else. For years, she had only partially lived her life outside of the campaign, always preoccupied. Maybe it was depression, she thought. Or exhaustion. Or both. Century had recently announced that in October it would close its Hawesville smelter until conditions were more favorable. If losing the Ravenswood plant felt like getting knocked off her feet, the Hawesville closure felt like being kicked while she was down. She shouldn't let it get to her, she knew. But it was painful to think that Century would pull the plug on Hawesville after all the effort that had gone into securing the new contract. The company had already laid off nearly one hundred Hawesville employees, and this would add five hundred to their ranks. Century was quick to place blame for the decision: China was flooding the aluminum market and sending aluminum prices back to Great Recession levels. The company recorded a loss of $34 million in the second quarter of 2015, and its stock price had dropped to under $5 per share. Karen, now religiously following manufacturing news and forecasts, worried that the outlook for the entire industry was bleak.

Near the Westin Hotel in downtown Chicago, Karen stood smoking a cigarette and watching the stream of pedestrians move past her on the sidewalks. The retirees weren't picketing this year. Two years ago they had towed the inflatable "Fat Cat" along with them to Chicago and displayed it in front of Century's new headquarters. Karen remembered pedestrians reacting to the retirees with their signs and handbills as if they had been asking for spare change. The lack of concern was practiced, Karen understood. Now she wondered how many of these men and women were responsible for making decisions, like Century's executives, to reduce or terminate benefits, close operations, or lock out workers. If it was the best decision for a company's bottom line, what difference did it make that real people might suffer the consequences? The distance that management maintained between themselves and their workforce—physically, socially, and psychologically—made this possible, she knew, because she had spent five long years trying to bridge this divide.

Inside the hotel conference room, before her speech, Karen looked at Century's board, wondering if she would be able to get through to them. Something was different this time around. She considered that she felt welcomed at this meeting rather than tolerated. At the front of the room, the board members were seated on a small stage, elevating them by several feet, so that they looked down at Karen the way a judge looks down on a courtroom. Karen stood in front of them, wearing her blue jeans and bright blue T-shirt with the bloodred handprints.

"I want to acknowledge that this is a difficult time for your company," Karen told the men in suits staring back at her. "But I want you to think of the men and women in Jackson County, West Virginia, and what we've been through these last five years."

While the men facing her made at least six figures, there were retirees back home who had to work out how to cover their increasing health care, grocery, and electricity bills on $600–$1,600 monthly pensions and Social Security checks. They had watched Century move through high times and low ones, but it was unthinkable for the company to ask the retirees to continue suffering when Century had the assets on hand to make this right. Too many retirees, well into their senior years, had been financially strapped for far too long. Too many lives had been lost already.

"All these retirees want," Karen said, "is to live out the rest of their retirement with the security and dignity that every person in this country deserves." They wanted to not worry about going bankrupt if they fell ill or about how they would pay for lifesaving medications if they or a loved one should need them. Karen also reminded the board, again, that the retirees had only ever asked for *what they had already paid for*.

"What it comes down to," she said, "is that this is the only right thing to do. If you want this company to really prosper, you have to take care of this." She spoke with confidence and conviction, but there was a weariness beneath the surface. She was tired of making the same argument, as if to a child, at that age when children have to be reminded that their actions have consequences; when they learn empathy. Karen knew the men on stage were listening, and she could see that they heard her. But would they act? She had to believe that they had a conscience. That they were good people, at heart, in spite of the circumstances that connected her life to theirs.

After Karen took her seat the members of the board pushed back their chairs and stood up, as they had done in 2013 and 2011. She always addressed them near the close of the meeting, and she was glad because she always felt like collapsing afterward. The men moved from the small stage toward Karen and the retirees. Unlike previous years, Century's board members did not make a hurried exit but introduced themselves and shook hands with Les Shockey, Jim Weltner, John Morris, Hoot Gibson, and others. One man had tears in his eyes when he greeted Karen.

"I'm sorry," he told her, and she knew then that she had done what she came to do.

On the drive home, Karen considered that finally, Century's board members may have acknowledged that the Ravenswood retirees were deserving of respect and of the health benefits the company had agreed to provide them. How could someone shake a man's hand, look him in the eye, and then knock him down again? Karen remembered what she had been told before speaking to Century's board the first time. *You can't shame corporate America*. But these men weren't evil, she told herself. Sure, she had called Logan Kruger evil, but she had to practice what she preached. She had to focus on the fact that these board members were human beings, with beating hearts, just like the retirees.

Karen knew she could drive herself mad running through scenarios in her head of how the board might respond, but she couldn't focus on anything else. She spent the next three days pacing around her dining room table. With every day that passed her doubts increased. Maybe she hadn't stressed enough that action needed to be taken *now*. The retirees could not sit on the back burner any longer. Every hour that passed, she felt one hour closer to accepting that this was over. That the shareholders' meeting had been her last chance.

Eventually, she wrote an email to Bless. "We are appreciative that you spent a good deal of time in discussion at the annual shareholders' meeting about the retirees. It would be beyond interesting to just listen and see how this tragic event really resonates with those that have the power to correct it. I can't tell you how many times I have wondered about that very thing. I have a strong sense that you, Mike Bless, are really seeing the immorality of this decision very strongly and that you have a sense of understanding about our situation, as best as you could from a distance." She noted that industry reports placed Century in a better position than its competitors and that there was no more time to delay. "We want and need this resolved," she wrote, "and it is absolutely not fair, considerate, or responsible to drag it on for weeks that lead into months that lead into years. We need our benefits now just as you expect your benefits to be paid when you have earned them. The retirees have always been ready and willing to listen. We have made it as clear as we can that we want to resolve this on a respectable and friendly basis." She ended by saying, "I trust you when you say you are in discussion and research. Please trust me when I say that time is not our friend."

Three days later, US district judge John Copenhaver granted Century's request for a summary judgment, filed in February 2014. He ruled that the evidence presented in the case "clearly and unambiguously" proved that the benefits outlined in each contract between Century and the union only remained in effect for the duration of the contract. Regardless of what the retirees knew to be true, the court did not agree, and Century was under no legal obligation to reinstate retiree health plans. Although the USW would appeal the decision, Karen believed the lifeline that this court case had offered retirees was effectively severed. "What a sad day for America, and a very sad day for the retirees," she wrote in a Facebook post. "We were always raised to believe in the justice system and that truth and fairness would prevail. In reality, corporate America can afford to hire the best lawyers in the country—and in our case, the biggest liars, in my opinion!" The retirees had already largely given up on the court case, in theory, but it was one of those times when Karen didn't realize that she had been holding on to a possibility, until she lost hold of it. That was the trouble. Rationally, she would not have argued that they had a strong chance in court, not after how things had gone so far. But faith wasn't rational. After the judge's ruling, she willed herself to stay focused on the positive. They could still count on Mike Bless, she insisted, though mainly to herself.

"Don't you remember who stole your insurance?" she was asked more than once. Karen reminded critics that Kruger was at the helm then. She didn't put Bless in the same category, though she knew people thought she was a fool for believing that Bless cared about the retirees. Some laughed openly at her defense of Century's CEO, and there were occasions when her own doubts took hold, when she thought that they were right. Since the shareholders' meeting, she was having a hard time not spiraling into hopelessness. She wrote a candid email to Bless, saying "no matter how much I want to try to have faith, I always have a certain amount of doubt, or maybe I should call it fear, that this is all a game of some kind and I am the pawn. I try to be positive and I try even harder to be patient but I just get terrified at times and the pessimistic part of me takes hold." When it got bad, as it had been lately, Karen felt at war with herself and couldn't decide what was true and what wasn't. Had anything she'd done made a difference? Could she trust Bless? Why did Century's board continue to make promises but avoid any concrete action that could help the retirees?

On November 24, 2015, Reuters published an article questioning if the country was witnessing the end of domestic aluminum production, which had been declining since 2001. Just eight smelters remained in the US, from twenty-two at the industry's peak. Of these, only four were producing metal, and only two at full capacity. China now produced more than half of the world's commodity-grade aluminum and was exporting more than ever. US companies couldn't compete, the author argued, noting that all three of Century's plants were "in trouble." Century had recently shuttered one of three potlines at its Sebree facility. They brought Hawesville back online at 40 percent capacity, only to issue notice to Mount Holly that the plant would shut down at the end of the year if the company could not secure a more competitive power deal in South Carolina.

This could be the end of their campaign, the Retiree Committee knew. The USW would appeal Judge Copenhaver's ruling, but the retirees didn't expect the outcome to change. They discussed that potentially a class action suit could still be filed, but that could also take five to ten years to move through the courts. After years of dedicating herself to this fight, Karen owed it to herself and the retirees not to lose hope. That hope now rested in the hands of Century's board members, who would review the information they were supposedly gathering on the issue and make a decision. More than likely, though, the board would conclude that the domestic aluminum industry was collapsing and that there was not a penny that could be spared.

Chapter Ten

Century could never find enough money to repay what has truly been taken from us for so very long—our dignity and our peace of mind.

—Karen Gorrell

Settled: December 2015–October 2017

Karen had hoped to connect with Mike Bless by phone before Century's December 2015 board meeting, but with the Mount Holly plant's future in question, he had repeatedly postponed their call. Karen understood, she told him. She was following the news in South Carolina closely and had even written to a newspaper there, urging the local electricity company, Santee Cooper, and the government to find a solution that would keep the Mount Holly plant open. Karen understood concerns that the power deal Century wanted would raise costs for other ratepayers in the state. But so would Century's departure, she warned. "When Century closed down in Jackson County, our power rates skyrocketed because our power company lost the revenue that Century provided. We are still paying that increased rate today," she wrote in her letter to the editor. "What do we have to show for it? A shuttered aluminum plant, higher rates, high unemployment, and a devastated community."

Century announced in mid-December that layoffs in South Carolina would begin over the Christmas holiday. Days later, the company reached an agreement with the electric company that would keep the Mount Holly plant operational

Retirees on the day their settlement is approved by the court.

at 50 percent capacity. Afterward, Bless followed up with Karen, requesting a meeting with the Retiree Committee. Karen reminded herself that the last time Mike Bless was adamant that they meet in person, it wasn't because he had good news. However, this time, Bless said that the purpose of the meeting was to discuss retiree insurance. The board had finished their review and was ready to move forward. Bless had made the case to the board that settling with the Ravenswood retirees was the right decision. Not only was it right by the retirees, but a settlement would end the USW's appeal of the district court's summary judgment. Although the courts had sided with Century to date, the appeal remained a liability. A settlement could also mitigate the damage inflicted on Century's public image by the retirees' targeted and outspoken campaign.

Karen read and reread the email from Bless and felt numb. There were too many emotions to sort out. She was elated and flooded with optimism, like a rush of serotonin, yet she was also cautious. Don't go too far down that path toward happiness, her body seemed to be saying. You can't afford the fallout. When she would look back on this period later, it was blank. After the shareholders' meeting and the court's ruling in Century's favor, time had stopped.

The Retiree Committee met with Mike Bless in Charleston, West Virginia, early in 2016 to discuss retiree health insurance. Bless had invited an actuary to the meeting, and the group spent an hour talking over the retirees' ideas for a fair deal for their insurance. Bless told retirees what he anticipated to be the next course of action: Century's board would review what they had just discussed and then talk with the company's lawyers, who would initiate conversation with the USW and its lawyers. Official negotiations for a settlement would continue from there. Weeks passed before the Retiree Committee heard any news, and the news they heard wasn't good: Century's lawyers were not pleased with Bless for beginning discussions without them. Any further talk would have to occur with legal counsel present. Another roadblock. Another delay. Eventually a date for the meeting between Century, the USW, and the Retiree Committee was set for the first week of August 2016—still months away.

Karen asked that the Retiree Committee meet with the USW's team the day before the official negotiations with Century, and it wasn't long into their conversation that she felt a knot in her stomach. She had previously reached out to Tom Conway, USW International vice president, to remind him of the proposal the Retiree Committee had presented to Century's board by email. The retirees knew they would need both the union and Century to agree to their ideas. They also knew, from past experience, that it was a long shot—but then again, so was their entire campaign. Under Karen's skillful leadership, with unrelenting resolve the retirees had inserted themselves as a party of interest in this fight, equally deserving of space at the negotiating table, whereas traditionally, the union would have spoken for them and negotiated on their behalf.

"The way the VEBA [voluntary employees' beneficiary association] was set up in 2012, it didn't work," Karen had told Conway. "We have a second chance now, and we need to walk away with something we can live with, something that's actually going to make a difference for the retirees." She explained that the Retiree Committee had discussed the issue at length and come up with a number that they thought everyone could agree on. The retirees were counting on Century offering less than what was discussed in 2012, given the financial concerns plaguing the industry, and they wanted to be prepared. After many meetings, they settled on a dollar amount that could be multiplied by the number of years someone had been employed at the plant. The longer a person had worked, the higher the payout they would receive.

If Century agreed to the retirees' terms, the retirees could get a fair deal for less than what Century had agreed to pay in 2012, Karen explained. "We can drop the settlement price to $26 million. *But*—and this is the only way it works," she emphasized, "we need that money all at once. No VEBA." The Retiree Committee wanted a onetime payment from Century that went directly to the retirees. Then they could all be done with this, and move forward with their lives.

Sitting in the USW's office, listening to Conway briefing them in preparation for the meeting with Century, Karen understood the retirees wouldn't get the deal they most wanted. It was just a gut feeling, but she trusted it, her heart sinking. The retirees had no leverage now that Century had decided to close the Ravenswood plant, Karen knew. She feared the worst, suddenly.

Please, God, don't let this end up like the court case, she said to herself. *Don't let the lawyers screw this up.* She focused on Tom Conway, who looked so much like her dad it felt surreal to be in the room with him. He had the same gray hair. The same strong build. Broad shoulders. In this moment, feeling like the floor might collapse beneath her, there was a comfort in being reminded of her dad. Regardless of what happened tomorrow, she told herself, her dad would have been proud of her for not giving up. His *beautiful black haired baby girl,* following in his footsteps: raising hell and standing up for the little guy.

The next day, during the negotiation meeting at the USW offices in Pittsburgh, Century offered $20 million to fund a VEBA. The USW would manage the VEBA, and the Ravenswood retirees could apply for reimbursement of health-related expenses for as long as money remained in the account. Karen, before breaking down in tears, before telling Mike Bless that it wasn't enough, pressed for an additional $6 million to reimburse retirees for medical expenses they incurred over the last six years while they were without Century's insurance. The retirees had made too many sacrifices that were being written off, she argued. After the meeting, Century agreed to offer $3 million as back compensation, and Mike Bless called Karen to let her know the additional funding had been approved by the board. She was relieved, and grateful that in spite of her tears, she had spoken up.

The Retiree Committee met with the USW in early September 2016 to discuss the VEBA, and Karen left that meeting with the impression that the settlement documents could be submitted to the court in as little as two weeks. More than a month later, this was still pending, and Karen lived in a state of perpetual dread, fearing something would go wrong and the offer would be rescinded. She had expected to feel relief after an agreement had been reached, but the retirees had been this close once before. If the settlement fell apart again, she didn't know if she could keep herself from falling apart with it. She also recognized that after six years, what patience she still had was wearing thin. No one else seemed to treat this situation with any sense of urgency, she thought, as she wrote to the lawyers for Century and the USW asking for a status update in November 2016. Two beneficiaries had died in the last two months, she shared. "I just need someone, anyone, all of you, to make this happen as soon as is reasonably possible." She offered to do whatever was needed to help.

On February 10, 2017, the USW announced that the settlement agreement was official, though still pending court approval. On February 14, the Retiree Committee held a press conference at the USW Local 5668 Union Hall outside of Ravenswood. More than sixty retirees were joined by longtime supporters, including Wes Holden from Senator Rockefeller's office, Kim Good from Senator Manchin's office, and West Virginia secretary of state Natalie Tennant. As Karen stood onstage preparing to address the audience, she saw Ann McKinney enter the union hall and motioned for Ann to take a seat in the front. The room fell silent as Ann moved through the crowd. Her late husband, Sam McKinney, had died exactly six years ago. This was the first time Ann had been to the union hall since that evening when Sam had spoken about the fear and disappointment brought on by the loss of his health insurance.

Sam was one of seventy-six Century Aluminum retirees who had passed away since Century ended their insurance benefits, and Ann's presence was a somber reminder of the sacrifices this community had made. Yet in spite of the deaths, the delays, and disappointments, more than seven hundred surviving retirees and their spouses would be eligible to receive compensation from Century.

In her speech, Karen spoke of the challenges that the retirees had faced while working to secure this settlement. She also said that in time, the retirees and Century's executives and board members came to respect one another. That was the real victory, she would say later. The retirees didn't give up, and Century Aluminum had put $23 million on the table when they could have walked away without offering a dime. She quoted Mike Bless: providing insurance for the retirees was simply the right thing to do. Karen had insisted over the years that Bless and Century's board see this truth, and she led a campaign that kept the retirees' stories and memories in the public eye. Thanks to the dedication of the retirees who stood beside her at every step, and the individuals who supported their campaign, Karen said they had accomplished what many told her was impossible.

Tom Conway, USW International vice president, commended the retirees in the union's announcement of the settlement, calling the achievement a testament to their "solidarity and hard work." Wes Holden referred to Karen as "a twenty-first-century Mother Jones," saying she had made history with this campaign. Senator Manchin provided a written statement, shared by Kim Good, acknowledging Karen as the "fearless leader on behalf of the retirees who remained steadfast in her commitment to fight the wrongful termination of their healthcare." Mike Gorrell, in a rare interview, shared with Ann Ali of *The State Journal* that the sacrifices had been worth it, and he was as proud of his wife as a person could be.

During the spring of 2017, the Retiree Committee helped the USW with the tedious task of verifying and tracking down retiree addresses in an effort to ensure that every eligible retiree would receive notice of the settlement. Karen and Les Shockey spent hours a day on this work. Then in May, retirees and spouses of the Ravenswood plant were mailed notice of the proposed terms of the settlement: each Medicare-eligible retiree and spouse could receive $2,700 annually, for at least ten years, payable as reimbursements for eligible expenses, such as Medicare Part B premiums. Retirees under sixty-five could begin collecting this amount once they turned sixty-five. In addition, each person could apply for a onetime nontaxable payment of up to $5,000 for the reimbursement of health-care costs incurred since losing their insurance. If a retiree or their spouse was deceased, the surviving spouse could apply for $1,000 to reimburse medical expenses of the deceased person.

Karen had argued for establishing a retiree seat on the VEBA Committee to ensure retirees would have a voice in how the funds were managed. She went as far as to petition US district judge John Copenhaver to accept this provision as an amendment to the settlement agreement, though in time, she withdrew the request. She didn't want to delay the process any further, and she was assured that the retirees would be given an opportunity to provide input if there were cause for substantial changes to the agreement. Days and then weeks passed while Karen and the retirees waited. Finally, on August 14, 2017, Judge Copenhaver approved an official settlement between the USW and Century Aluminum. He called it "generous," given the court rulings to date. Karen wrote to Bless the night before the hearing to thank him, saying, "This never would have happened without a determined old lady and a CEO with a caring heart." The next month, when Century authorized the first payment to fund the VEBA trust, Bless shared with Karen that signing off on that payment was the proudest moment in his career.

The Retiree Committee held a celebration picnic at the Ravenswood union hall in early October 2017. The heavy heat of late summer had subsided, but it was still T-shirt weather, and the sun shone bright in a blue sky with a whisper of clouds.

The leaves on the trees surrounding the open field next to the union hall were half green and half shades of yellow and orange. More than one hundred people sat in lawn chairs or folding chairs beneath tents or in the shade of the outbuildings on the property. The attendees were retirees of Century Aluminum, or their family members, or friends and supporters. A band played to kick off the event, as guests were arriving, then Karen and the retirees took the stage. Just the top third of Karen's torso and her head cleared the extra-large podium, painted sky blue and bearing the USW emblem. She looked out on the crowd from behind tinted glasses, her short dark hair highlighted with light blond streaks. On either side of Karen stood the other members of the Retiree Committee: Hoot Gibson, Jim Weltner, John Morris, Ripcord Dixon (with Betty Jane), Les Shockey, and Mel Lawrence. A large hand-painted "Fort Unity" sign still adorned the roof of the stage, and below, the retirees hung a poster board sign—one of many placed around the event—with the words "It takes a village. Thank you for being a part of ours."

After turning toward the flag at the stage's back corner for the Pledge of Allegiance and a prayer by Bill Stephens, Karen began her long list of acknowledgments. First, she thanked two women who she said had sacrificed more than anyone should have to sacrifice, inviting the wives of Bryce Turner and Sam McKinney to the stage. The two women, Cindy Turner and Ann McKinney, walked up the stairs together and were met with hugs and tears. Karen welcomed Governor Tomblin, Secretary of State Natalie Tennant, Wes Holden, Sherry Breeden, and USW staff and leadership to the stage. Karen invited the other members of her "army" to join her—the men and women who had attended years of meetings, pickets, protests, and events, culminating in the settlement. Each person was given the opportunity to speak and presented with a commemorative

Karen and retirees on the Fort Unity stage during the settlement celebration picnic.

coin engraved with two images that, for Karen, were emblematic of their long battle for health benefits: an image of the Occupy camp showing the white camper and tents, and a second image of Larry Williams, with his cane, handing a flyer to a passing car. The text on the coin read "Century Aluminum Retirees, Fighting for Justice. We Kept Our Promise."

Insured: October 2017–November 2018

In the fall of 2017, Karen was admitted to the hospital for pneumonia. After being released, she arrived home to find the paperwork from the settlement had arrived. For years, she had promised her family—and Larry Williams, who bugged her about it repeatedly—that she would quit smoking when she got her health insurance from Century. It had been a way to avoid the issue at the time, when she knew that she was far too stressed to consider quitting. But in the hospital, she had been too sick to smoke, and she took that as a sign, throwing out what was left in her pack before taking her and Mike's application to enroll in the VEBA to the mailbox. She would keep this promise, too, she told herself.

Karen and Mike Gorrell's application was approved, and they received their back pay compensation from the settlement by year's end. Karen and the other committee members also received a modest reimbursement for their time and travel expenses. As documentation, they each submitted a travel log notating their trips throughout West Virginia, Kentucky, Ohio, South Carolina, California, Pennsylvania, and Illinois. It was impressive to see the scope of the six-year, multistate campaign, organized by a group of volunteer retirees, led by a woman with no previous labor or campaign experience. These individuals had established a network of supporters that stretched across the country and had won the favor of state and federal representatives and, eventually, the CEO and board of Century Aluminum.

After the settlement, Karen and the Retiree Committee continued to hold meetings every other week at the union hall, providing retirees an opportunity to ask questions and receive assistance with the paperwork they were required to submit each quarter in order to receive their reimbursement payments from the VEBA. The meetings also provided a forum for Karen to share updates with retirees, as she stepped into the role of unofficial liaison between the VEBA trust administrators and beneficiaries. By the time the first payment had been authorized, Karen was already fielding questions from retirees, and as much as she might get on the last nerve of the trust administrators, she told herself she had to stay involved. In lieu of having a retiree serve on the trust committee, the only way Karen knew to ensure that retirees' interests were considered was if she spoke up for them. She asked to review the letters mailed to retirees, and as she had throughout this journey, she continued to advocate for the interests of the older retirees. "I just want it to be fairer to those that suffered so very much for so long," she wrote to a trust administrator in one of her emails. "Please try and understand our point. I just hate seeing these older guys lose out on any more than they already have."

More than two dozen retirees gathered for one of the biweekly settlement meetings in November 2018. This particular meeting began with the announcement that there was a card to sign for Roy Daly, a retiree scheduled for open-heart surgery. Bill Stephens led the group in prayer. As Roy's card was passed around the tables and signed, Karen spoke about the Medicare Advantage Plan that was now being offered through the VEBA. Many retirees had questions about the plan, which they could elect to receive in place of the annual reimbursement.

"If you got this letter and you don't want to apply for the insurance, you don't have to do anything," Karen announced. "If you don't want the plan, don't send the form back, because you wouldn't want to check the wrong box and then find out you enrolled in a plan you don't want to be enrolled in." Worrying about retirees filling out the paperwork the settlement required kept Karen up at night. She was relieved that retirees now had the option to enroll in an insurance plan, because she knew people were struggling with the reimbursement forms, which could be cumbersome. Rather than calling the trust administrators, many retirees called Karen or the others volunteering with her. Karen had recently spent forty-five minutes on the phone with a retiree and wasn't sure the man understood anything more clearly at the end of it. She preferred that retirees came to these meetings so that they could fill out their forms with someone on hand to assist them.

"Well, do you think it's a good deal or not?" Larry Williams asked about the Advantage Plan. Karen explained that each person would have to look at the details of their current plan and the details of this offer, and for the next fifteen minutes, the retirees discussed the differences. The cost difference could amount to several thousand dollars a year, so it was important to make an informed decision.

"What tears me up is the prescriptions," someone shared. There were affirmations from the crowd. Karen said that's what gets everyone. She knew retirees who were still spending more than $1,000 a year on medications, even now. She couldn't imagine what they were paying before.

Karen also spoke to the retirees about the money that remained of the $3 million allocated for the reimbursement of expenses incurred while the retirees went without insurance—the $5,000 per person. Karen had pushed for retirees to receive additional compensation if they still had outstanding expenses, since there was still money in the pot. She argued to the VEBA trust committee that many retirees had spent more than $10,000 just in insurance premiums during the years they went without Century's insurance. Karen knew several people who had spent $30,000–$40,000 on health-related expenses in that time. In just one year, Les Shockey paid over $10,000 out of pocket to cover the costs related to his wife's cancer treatment. Because she passed away before the settlement, he could only claim $1,000 of her total medical expenses for reimbursement. Karen was willing to keep fighting, though she listened to those who advised her to let it go, determining that whatever extra money they might receive wouldn't be worth the fight to get it.

It was hard for Karen to want to give this up, on principle, but she accepted that her companions were right. There were many people, like Les Shockey, who had paid out far more for health expenses than they would receive in compensation, but they weren't walking away empty handed. The painful disappointment that Karen felt when she first heard Century's offer had faded over time. A $23 million settlement was an incredible achievement. It was true that it was less than the $44 million on the table in 2012, but Karen had to consider that the 2012 deal had included retirees under sixty-five as beneficiaries, which added to the overall cost. The deal they got wasn't perfect, but it still felt miraculous now that her intense emotions had subsided.

For the retirees and families who benefited from this settlement, the money was life-changing, Karen knew. She and Mike were grateful to be putting the years of worry and stress behind them. They were grateful to have a little more financial security and to be able to access the health care they needed, when they needed it, without making sacrifices because of gaps in coverage or out-of-pocket costs they had to pay with their Medicare plans.

Karen knew, too, that no matter what happened next, she had kept her promise to Bryce Turner and to Sam McKinney. Karen needed to remind herself of that from time to time. She needed to stay focused on the positive, because for as much relief as she felt, she now had days when she didn't know what to do with herself. The campaign had consumed so much of her time and energy that she felt the absence of it like the loss of a loved one. It had taken up that kind of space in her life.

What was clear was that she remained grateful for her "silver-haired army," as she now called them—the men and women who had stood by her side for the better part of a decade. They had witnessed her at her lowest and at her best. She still gave the Retiree Committee grief for letting her sob at the last negotiation meeting without handing her a tissue.

Hoot said he had been in shock seeing Karen's sudden loss of composure. Even those closest to her hadn't known the full weight that she carried emotionally. She knew without a doubt, though, that she wouldn't have gotten beyond writing letters and making phone calls if it hadn't been for these retirees. At their celebration picnic, someone had told Karen that they thought one of the more remarkable parts of the campaign was that the group still liked each other and hadn't splintered after doing this work for so many years. Karen responded that in fact, they loved each other, and that love had only strengthened over time.

In the year following the settlement, Karen and the retirees continued to meet regularly, and were asked to speak on occasion to groups of college students visiting West Virginia as part of their school's service-learning programs. The trips were organized by Tom Breiding, working for the Appalachian Institute, then affiliated with Wheeling Jesuit University. Karen had initially reached out to Tom, a songwriter known for his work with the United Mineworkers Union, asking if he would consider writing a song to memorialize the retirees' victory. He wrote about the retirees' fight as a David versus Goliath battle, and the lyrics gave Karen chills each time she listened. When Tom invited the retirees to share their story with the students he hosted, Karen agreed, though she wasn't sure how well the retirees' story would go over with college students.

"I feel as nervous as I did talking to the bigwigs at Century," Karen admitted to her companions on the way to their first talk. These kids were thinking of their first jobs and internships, not retirement. They also came from prestigious schools and lived all over the United States, as far away as California, Karen learned. Their lives were far removed from the factories and coal fields of West Virginia, and they were more likely to be the future CEOs of companies than to work blue collar union jobs. Karen's insecurities, which she thought she had put behind her, were surfacing again—what did she have to say that these kids could possibly care about?

At one of these meetings, in the fall of 2018, Karen and several retirees and their wives sat in a row of chairs at the back of the union hall in Ravenswood, facing two dozen college students from two private universities in the Midwest. Karen introduced herself and each person seated with her and explained how the men onstage had worked all their lives as union members, only to have their retirement benefits revoked suddenly without union negotiations. She stopped then to survey the crowd with questions: Had anyone grown up in a union family? No one had. She asked if anyone knew anything about unions. If they had heard of the nineteenth-century labor organizer Mother Jones, by chance. The students responded with blank stares, while Les Shockey and John Morris exchanged surprised looks with one another. Karen hadn't prepared herself for this. She didn't have time to go into the history of unions, she said, but was adamant that the students learn it. "There is so much that we all take for granted," she told them, "that men and women have fought tooth and nail to make a reality." She said this because even she had taken her husband's benefits for granted. Even after hearing of other unions, other retirees, who had their benefits slashed, Karen didn't think to speak up or take any action. Then it was her benefits, and it was devastating.

"I was just a grandma from West Virginia," she told the students. "And with these retirees, we stood up to one of the largest aluminum companies in this country—a company backed by one of the biggest multinational corporations on the planet." Karen wanted to make the point that a person didn't need any special qualifications to choose to do the right thing. Or, as her dad would say, to fight for the little guy. Before starting this journey, she said she had never been politically active and insisted that it was never too late to stand up for what was right. Or, she thought, *it's never too soon*, looking at the faces of the students in front of her. Karen said she was impressed with today's youth, who she watched on the news speaking out about gun violence after multiple school shootings had shocked and shattered communities across the United States. Each event broke Karen's heart and she was glad to see young people taking a stand. She told the students in front of her that she cared about their futures because she cared about her grandchildren and great grandchildren's futures. Those futures were worth fighting for, and sadly, Karen said, it looked like they would have to fight.

"I hope one of you kids does go out and pick up the cross and work from your heart," she told them. "That's how we won our battle—we put our hearts into it, and we wouldn't let anybody keep us down."

Governor Earl Ray Tomblin stands with Karen and Mike Gorrell at the celebration picnic.

Epilogue

Karen Gorrell should be remembered as the Mother Jones of this century. To paraphrase Winston Churchill: never have so many owed so much to so few. That's the truth about what Karen and these retirees did for their union.

—Wes Holden

2018–2024

For two years after their settlement, Karen and the Retiree Committee continued hosting biweekly meetings for retirees at the Ravenswood union hall and continued to meet with visiting groups of college students when asked to speak about their campaign. In 2020, as social distancing restrictions were put in place during the COVID-19 pandemic, these meetings and speaking events ended abruptly. For the first time in a decade, the retirees canceled their Christmas celebration. Since then, Karen's "retiree army" has lost four members—Sonny Hinzman, Les Shockey, Larry Williams, and Lois Gibson. Karen was diagnosed with chronic obstructive pulmonary disease and has struggled with health challenges. She's not able to get around as well as she used to.

Karen has remained connected with many people she met during her campaign, counting many of the retirees' supporters as friends. She is Facebook friends with former and current state representatives and union leaders. She has kept in touch with Sherry Breeden, Wes Holden, John Beaver, and others, including Mike Bless, who retired from Century in 2021. Though they see each other less often since the pandemic disrupted their meetings, Karen keeps in contact with her retiree family: Jim Weltner, Bill Stephens, Ripcord and Betty Jane Dixon, John and Mary Morris, and others. She also continues to field the occasional question from retirees about the voluntary employees' beneficiary association (VEBA) paperwork, though the number of calls has decreased. Nevertheless, every year, retirees or their spouses who turn sixty-five years old become eligible to enroll in the VEBA, and it's still known that they can contact Karen or other volunteers if they need assistance. Karen has remained an advocate for the retirees, working with a trusted contact with the VEBA who can help her solve problems when they arise, such as an application being denied because a retiree fills out the paperwork incorrectly.

Other than this support role, Karen has stepped back from her work as an organizer, returning to her nana duties. At the time of this writing, in August 2024, Karen and Mike spend as much time as they can with their children and grandchildren. They welcomed their first great-grandchild to the family in December 2019. That same year, Karen's daughter and son-in-law opened a restaurant, where Karen works at the front counter a few evenings a week. There she gets to spend time with her daughter's family and, occasionally, will get to meet retirees who benefited from the settlement.

"Are you the woman who fought for our insurance from Century?" a man asked Karen as he and his wife were leaving the restaurant in December 2022. The couple, Dave and Judy Powers, recognized Karen's face from newspaper photos but had not met her in person.

"Yes, that's me," Karen admitted.

"We can't thank you enough," the man said, putting his hand to his heart. The couple shared that Judy was diagnosed with cancer after Century cut off their insurance. It was challenging, but since the settlement, the couple felt like they could manage. They were able to focus their attention on Judy's care and recovery rather than how they would pay for it. The total costs for her treatment were unbelievably high. Karen understood, she told them. She thanked God every day for the settlement and especially on days when medical bills arrived in the mail. Karen had recently spent three days in the hospital. The cost of that visit, before the settlement, would have upended the Gorrells' finances had they relied on Medicare alone.

By 2024, Karen estimates that she and Mike, and other couples, have received somewhere around $50,000 from the settlement, between the initial back pay and the annual reimbursements over seven years. Considering the cost of living and the amount of their pension and Social Security income, it's a substantial amount of money. Then there was the money they saved through the supplemental insurance policies retirees purchased, and the peace of mind that came with knowing they wouldn't have to worry about the financial burden of receiving medical care. The latter has had an immense effect on Karen's mental health, and that value can't be easily measured. When Karen considers this or thinks of the stories she's heard from other retirees, it is a welcomed reminder of the positive impact that her small, committed group of retirees have had on their community.

Acknowledgments

I am deeply grateful for each person who contributed to the content of this book. Thank you to John Morris, Les Shockey, Jim Weltner, Bill Stephens, Luther "Hoot" Gibson, Lois Gibson, Ron "Ripcord" Dixon, and Betty Jane Dixon for taking the time to answer my questions and to read a draft of the manuscript. I extend the same thanks to John Beaver, Mike Bless, Sherry Breeden, Jodi Damron, Chad Gorrell, Wes Holden, and Ann McKinney for their time and for expanding my understanding and perspective. The investment of time and interest from these individuals made this work possible.

This book has also benefited greatly from the attention of three peer reviewers who identified specific opportunities to improve the content and structure of the manuscript and who encouraged its publication. Their feedback and questions have made this a better story. I am very appreciative of the time that several people spent reading all or sections of the manuscript, including Tom Breiding, Holly Weigman, Molly Cox, and Mary Forfia. John Beaver, Betsy Bethel McFarland, and Stacie Leone each read a complete draft and offered detailed feedback that improved the final version of this book. Katie O'Neill read multiple drafts, providing thoughtful comments and encouragement as the book evolved. I am grateful to these readers and others who believed in this story and who supported its long path to publication.

I am fortunate to know Eddy Pendarvis and benefited from her support and advice when I was searching for a publisher, including her edits of the manuscript and proposal and her introduction to Mountain State Press. A thank-you also is due to Cat Pleska, of Mountain State Press, who believed this book had potential and who put me in contact with the University Press of Kentucky (UPK), where it would find a home. Abby Freeland, at UPK, has been instrumental in this book's development, and I am grateful for her guidance and for her ongoing work on the book's behalf. UPK's director, Ashley Runyon, also provided feedback that improved the manuscript. I thank Abby and Ashley and the editorial and production team at UPK for their work to bring this book into the world. I also want to acknowledge Abby and UPK's commitment to extending publishing opportunities to individuals from communities whose stories have often been excluded from history, literature, and popular culture. I believe this effort is having a positive effect within the Appalachian region and beyond.

This book has benefited from the work of several journalists whose coverage of the retirees' story over the years provided a wealth of information that helped me piece together a timeline of events and fill in important details and context. Specifically, Jared Hunt, Paul Nyden, and Ann Ali were dedicated to keeping the retirees' efforts in print. I am also grateful for James Fassinger's coverage of the retirees' Occupy camp and their time in Chicago. The photos and videos he captured added depth to my understanding of the retirees' efforts. Many thanks are also due to Jesse Thorton for his help preparing many of the photos in the book for publication and answering my photo questions.

I am appreciative of my time working for Aimee and Craig Howley and Berkeley Franz while I wrote the initial drafts of this book. Their work as authors and researchers was influential. A debt of gratitude is also owed to Kelsi Boyd for offering me a home in West Virginia when I committed to finishing this book and for her patience when it took years to do so! I am grateful for my friendship with Tom Breiding, whose music and dedication to sharing stories of Appalachian labor organizing have been an inspiration. I am also grateful for the connections I have made in the last two years with other writers through West Virginia Writers Inc. and the Appalachian Writers Workshop in Hindman, Kentucky. I have been inspired and encouraged by these relationships. And I am grateful always to my parents for their lifelong encouragement and support.

My deepest thanks to Karen Gorrell for inspiring this work and for trusting me to tell this story. The time and effort Karen spent cataloging and documenting the retirees' campaign as it happened were a tremendous resource that supported this writing. I am also grateful for the hours she spent answering questions during our interviews and later as I was working on edits. I am grateful for her reading multiple drafts of the manuscript, for connecting me to several individuals I interviewed, and for living a life that inspires others.

Finally, I want to acknowledge that the contributions and sacrifices of many people who worked on this campaign far exceeded what I've captured in these pages. There were also many people who were influential to Karen and to this campaign who were not mentioned in this book (or only mentioned briefly) but who deserve acknowledgment, including the following Ravenswood retirees: A. G. Brilhart, Bob Blaire, Harold "BamBam" Boggess, Roy Dailey, Betty Jane Dixon, Gene Fowler, Sonny Hinzman, Bob Holland, Charlie King, Mac McDaniel, Mary Morris, Gene Nutter, Roland Price, Sharon Price, Jean Stephens, Naomi Shockey, Sally Taylor, Faye Skeen, Walter "Peach" Skeen, Coy Wade, Drucilla Wade, and Frank West. And, from Hawesville, Kentucky, Preston Blake, Richard Frye, Andy Meserve, and Pete Shouse. My sincere apologies to anyone I have omitted from this list.

Appendix

Artifacts

The following are samples of materials created by Karen Gorrell for the retirees' campaign.

Retiree's Lives Are In Century's Hands

Published by Century Aluminum Retirees February 17th, 2011 Volume 1 Issue 1

CENTURY ALUMINUM ROBBING HEALTHCARE FROM DEDICATED RETIREES

On November 1st, 1990, Ravenswood Aluminum (Currently Century Aluminum) made the decision to LOCK OUT 1700 Steelworkers in a blatant attempt to bust the union. The lockout and ramifications from it had a devastating effect on the workers, their families and the entire community of Jackson County and surrounding counties as well. The once peaceful and family oriented community found itself in the middle of a very long and ugly battle that divided families, churches and neighborhoods; and was often violent and destructive to all that were involved. This was just a signal of the ruthlessness this company would exercise in years to come. The company's only regret was that the union lasted "One Day Longer" and won the battle and the dedicated steelworkers reclaimed their jobs. **Once again, Century Aluminum's Corporate greed has raised it's ugly head!!** They have made the decision to terminate the contractually promised healthcare coverage of the retirees that have dedicated decades of service to the company, creating huge profits over the years. Now that these retirees are of no value to Century, they have been cast aside like garbage, many of them facing their golden years with absolutely no health care in their most vulnerable years. Each and every retiree decided to take retirement largely based on Century's agreement to provide healthcare until their death. ***Killing off seniors by robbing access to basic healthcare should be criminal and MUST be stopped!!***

CENTURY ALUMINUM CEO COMPENSATIONS

Century Aluminum's spokesman, Mr. Dildine, according to a recent news article in the Charleston Gazette, stated that terminating the contractually promised retiree healthcare benefit was a necessary action to insure profitability of the Ravenswood facility. The retiree healthcare was a contractual benefit that the union members made wage and other concessions over the years to insure. Maybe he should have stated the following information located on the Forbes web site:

LOGAN W. KRUGER
Director, President and Chief Executive Officer
Century Aluminum Corporation
Total Compensation 2009
$4,196,396.00

MICHAEL A. BLESS
Executive Vice President and Chief Financial Officer
Century Aluminum Corporation
Total Compensation 2009
$1,622,475.00
(Just 2 of many!)

If they really want to cut cost and insure profitability to the Ravenswood operations, then it is their salaries that need terminated!

MANY CENTURY RETIREES HAVE LIFE-THREATENING ILLNESSES

Many of the affected retirees are suffering from severe and disabling medical conditions that are life threatening and require intense medical treatment. Many of these ailments are likely a direct result of many decades of service to Century Aluminum and it's affiliates. Bryce Turner, retiree, is currently fighting the ultimate battle after being diagnosed with leukemia. In February 2010, after exploring his options, Bryce submitted his application for retirement, based largely on the assurance that he, along with his wife, would have healthcare until their death. "When you are in a critical care facility 4 hours from home, all the worrisome issues regarding health, money, and emotional distress, arrangements for home and family in your absence, etc. that must be dealt with can be quite overwhelming. My wife and I were greatly comforted by the fact that we had such good health insurance to cover my new extremely high medical expenses. But now the harsh, sudden, and unforeseen retraction of those retirement benefits will have a devastating effect on many people."

Century Aluminum is depriving retirees of life sustaining care in exchange for PROFIT!

Newsletter #1.

Retiree's Lives Are In Century's Hands

Published by Century Aluminum Retirees June 4th, 2011 Volume 1 Issue 2

CENTURY ALUMINUM RETIREES TRAVEL FROM WEST VIRGINIA TO MONTEREY, CALIFORNIA TO PROTEST TERMINATION OF PROMISED RETIREE HEALTH CARE BENEFITS

We have traveled to California in protest of the unilateral termination of contractually promised retiree health care by Century Aluminum. This callous decision has placed unspeakable devastation on several hundred retirees and their spouses. The obligation by Century to provide retiree health care until death has been a benefit promised and practiced for decades. A percentage of the employees hourly wage was designated for retiree health care coverage over the years. Having to purchase health care insurance was not a factor considered by the employees as they did their financial planning for retirement because we believed that Century would honor their obligations. America's most vulnerable citizens have been pushed over the cliff without life sustaining health care, all in the name of profit!

It is impossible to describe the devastation this decision has caused the retirees and their families. There are retirees that are no longer taking necessary medications due to the exorbitant cost to purchase them. One retiree in particular, Sam McKinney, passed away on February 14, 2011, after attending a meeting to discuss efforts to wage this battle with Century Aluminum to try and restore our promised health care. He was under a tremendous amount of stress related to the loss of his wife's health care and his inability to provide the health care she would so desperately need. His monthly pension was approximately $600.00 and when he passed, his wife's survivor benefit was reduced to $300.00. Sam was a good Christian man and worked hard all of his life to purchase a modest home and save a few dollars. Without forfeiting most of her assets, his wife will not qualify for any medical assistance. No one could ever comprehend the stress this callous decision has caused and that in itself, is life threatening to many of us. It feels like Murder without a Gun! Where are Century's ethics?

"CENTURY ALUMINUM RETIREES MAY HAVE ONE FOOT IN THE GRAVE, BUT WE ARE DETERMINED TO KICK LIKE HECK WITH THE OTHER!"

.Century Aluminum obviously misjudged the passion of the aging retirees to fight for our lives. Many of the affected retirees are too sick to stand on picket lines or travel to California, but the ones of us that are able represent those that are not. We are determined not to lose any more retirees due to the stress caused by the loss of health care or their inability to seek even routine medical treatment. We did not work all of our lives to lose all that we own without a fight. We have tremendous support from our state and our community and the support is growing daily! Our trip to California was financed by our community, co-workers, and caring groups across our state. Our US Senator has pledged to be our voice in this battle and has taken our case to Washington. We vow to never give up until justice is served and the health care we were promised is reinstated.

We are not wealthy in worldly goods, but we are rich in morals and determination. We are volunteers, veterans, preachers, Sunday school teachers, and nanas and papas and we deserve better than to be tossed aside by corporate America with an insatiable quest for profit. Many of the annual executive compensations for Century are in the multi-million dollar range and growing. In a recently filed Form 8-K document, Century posted earnings of 25 million in the first quarter of 2011. They state changes (which should be called terminations, in our opinion) to the Century of West Virginia retiree medical benefits program increased quarterly results by $9.4 million with an associated discrete tax benefit of $2.1 million. Century indicates they are working to restart the Ravenswood, WV facility and they are seeking lucrative power contracts and tax breaks from our state in order to insure their profitability!

It seems apparent that profit takes precedence over human life and dignity! We worked very hard to inform our legislators about the devastation Century has placed upon us and were successful in killing a bill that would have possibly saved them millions of dollars on their power bill if a restart is actually performed. They were given the option of restoring health care and declined and the bill died in the Finance Committee. We promise to be on every corner until we secure the benefit we paid for-our retiree health care!

Newsletter #2.

Century Aluminum Retirees

Ravenswood, West Virginia By: Karen Gorrell **September 6, 2011**

Century Aluminum Retirees Standing Together!!! We may have one foot in the grave, but we will fight like heck with the other!! Contact us at proudlilnana @suddenlink .net

Century Aluminum Retirees Contractually Promised Health Care Benefits Terminated!

Over 500 families have been devastated by Century Aluminum's unlawful termination of contractually promised health care benefits. These benefits were paid for by decades of service and many concessions were made over the years to insure them. On January 1, 2010, Century terminated health care for most all post 65 retirees and agreed to continue coverage for early retirees until age 65 and Medicare eligible. On January 1, 2011, Century dropped the final ax by terminating the early retiree benefits. The cost to replace supplemental health care and prescription benefits coverage have exceeded the entire pension benefits of many retirees, eliminating their basic living income from their budget. Most pre 65 retirees have pre-existing conditions, and are unable to pay the cost of full health care premiums, placing all of their life long acquired assets at risk and jeopardizing their ability to obtain quality care.

Stress Kills! We Have Already Lost A Few Good Men!!

On February 14, 2011, Sam McKinney, retiree, attended a retiree meeting about the loss of his health care benefits. Sam had previously had a heart attack and was not a well man. The devastation of losing his health care benefits for himself and his spouse was foremost on his mind. He had recently taken his very sick and pre 65 wife to apply for medical assistance and had been turned down. He worked hard all of his life and purchased a modest home and saved a few dollars and because of that, no help was available. His pension was barely $600.00 per month. The stress was overwhelming and showed clearly that day. As he later drove to town for a Valentines dinner with his wife, he commented to her about how he knew when he married her, he could take care of her and how Century had stolen that ability from him. He told her if something would happen to him, he didn't know who would take care of her. Sam had a massive heart attack and died that day in the parking lot of the restaurant!

Retirees Seek Senator Rockefeller and Senator Manchin's Help In Sponsoring Legislation To Stop This Outrageous Devastation By Corporate America!

As CEO compensations continue to rise in the multi million dollar ranges, corporate America appears willing to sacrifice their retirees to improve their profit line! Human life and dignity of retirees seems to be of no consequence in exchange for the rich to become richer! As we witness the attack on Medicare and Social Security, seniors must realize the extremes the rich and powerful will strive for at the cost of America's most vulnerable citizens. As we fight to preserve these programs, let us also fight to enact legislation to protect retiree benefits secured by ratified union contracts. Unscrupulous corporations like Century Aluminum are making a mockery of their obligations and too many courts uphold them! Ask your legislators to preserve retiree benefits and support legislation to insure this doesn't happen to you!!

Alliance for Retired Americans event flyer.

The *Century Aluminum Retirees* Invite

You To Join Them In The

<u>"REOPENING OF FORT UNITY"</u>

<u>August 27 12:00 Noon-3:00</u>

Location: Local 5668 Union Hall
Ravenswood,WV

Century Aluminum Unilaterally Terminated The Contractually Promised and Life Sustaining Health Care Benefits Of Retirees

WE ARE FIGHTING BACK!!

WE NEED <u>YOUR</u> SUPPORT!!

Bring a Covered Dish and Enjoy
Guest Speakers, Live Music,

Good Food and Fellowship!

(Meat and Soft Drinks Will Be Provided)

Bring your lawn chair, friends, and family! Help us fill that hillside with support!

IT IS OUR HEALTH CARE TODAY—IT COULD BE YOURS TOMORROW!!

Reopening Fort Unity flyer.

Notes

I interviewed Karen for the first time in March 2018 and again in February, May, July, and November 2019. In 2019, I also interviewed John Morris, Jim Weltner, Les Shockey, and Wes Holden. I relied on these interviews, as well as emails, letters, Facebook posts, flyers, handbills, and news articles, to draft the first version of this manuscript. In 2024, after receiving feedback on the manuscript from peer reviewers, I interviewed Mike Bless, John Beaver, Ripcord and Betty Dixon, Jodi Damron, and Chad Gorrell and expanded sections of the text to include their experiences and perspectives. In 2024, I also spoke with Sherry Breeden, Hoot and Lois Gibson, Bill Stephens, and Ann McKinney to verify and fill in details about their lives. (I reached out to others but did not get a response.) When the manuscript was near completion, I shared a draft of the story (or relevant sections) with interviewees and gave them the opportunity to offer feedback or corrections. What follows is a summary of sources referenced for each chapter.

Preface

Epigraph

West Virginia secretary of state Natalie Tennant, email to Century Aluminum CEO Logan Kruger, February 17, 2011.

Office of Senator John D. Rockefeller, press release, February 29, 2012.

Karen Gorell, interview with author, March 2018

Chapter One

Epigraph

Office of Senator John D. Rockefeller, press release, June 3, 2014.

Enough

The opening scene was recounted by Karen and Mike Bless and is supplemented by details from interviews with other retirees (John Morris, Jim Weltner, Ripcord). Karen's life story and information about her family were informed by multiple interviews with her.

Kaiser and the Ravenswood Aluminum Company

The history of the Ravenswood plant was informed by interviews with Karen, the book *Ravenswood,* and the articles listed here. Population information came from census records accessed online. Details about events leading to the lockout and relations between the union and the plant as well as the union's tactics were informed by the book *Ravenswood.*

Juravich, Tom, and Kate Bronfenbrenner. *Ravenswood: The Steelworkers' Victory and the Revival of American Labor.* Ithaca, NY: Cornell University Press, 1999.

"Kaiser Produces First Aluminum in Valley." *Ravenswood News,* November 21, 1957. https://archive.wvculture.org/history/businessandindustry/kaiseraluminum01.html

"Look Homeward Angel." Kaiser Aluminum News, Summer 1958. https://archive.wvculture.org/history/businessandindustry/kaiseraluminum03.html

"Plant Production Started—Editors See History Made at New Plant." *Jackson Herald,* November 22, 1957. https://archive.wvculture.org/history/businessandindustry/kaiseraluminum02.html

Walters, Donna. "How the Former Kaiser Companies Have Fared: Aluminum Operations Are Cut Back in Hopes Move Will Stimulate Growth." *Los Angeles Times*, August 4, 1985.

Lockout

Karen supplied the details about her life at this time, including recounting the incident with a replacement worker, her involvement with the Women's Support Group, and the stress she experienced. Her son, Chad, contributed additional details about the events involving him. Details about the union's tactics and the final negotiations primarily came from the book *Ravenswood* and the other sources listed here.

Heilprin, J. "Financier Marc Rich Dies in Switzerland." *San Diego Union-Tribune*, June 26, 2013.

Juravich, Tom, and Kate Bronfenbrenner. *Ravenswood: The Steelworkers' Victory and the Revival of American Labor*. Ithaca, NY: Cornell University Press, 1999.

Kilborn, P. T. "How a Union Won an Appalachian Struggle." *New York Times*, May 8, 1992.

Presley Noble, B. "At Work; Different Tactics in Labor's Battles." *New York Times*, September 6, 1992.

Chapter Two

Epigraph

Karen Gorrell, Century Aluminum retirees handbill, June 2011.

Retirement

Karen recounted the story of Mike's hospitalization and talked at length about how the retirees were impacted by the loss of health insurance plans. Karen also provided copies of benefits documents, the termination letter Mike received, and documents detailing the wage and benefits contribution amounts from past union negotiations, which she had collected during her campaign. Interviews with retirees (Les Shockey, Jim Weltner, John Morris) expanded my understanding of how individuals were affected by the loss of insurance. Details about the plant closing and the termination of insurance plans came from the news articles listed here. Details about the cost burden of Medicare came from the Kaiser Family Foundation report.

Associated Press. "Century Aluminum: Closing to Cost $30M." *Parkersburg News and Sentinel*, February 12, 2009.

Associated Press. "Century Aluminum Retirees Outraged over Benefit Cuts." *Charleston Gazette-Mail*, November 13, 2010.

Baidya, Atish. "Officials Meet to Discuss Future of Plant." WOWK-TV, January 10, 2009.

Cubanski, Juliette, Christina Swoope, Anthony Damico, and Tricia Neuman. "How Much Is Enough? Out-of-Pocket Spending among Medicare Beneficiaries: A Chartbook." Kaiser Family Foundation, 2014. https://www.kff.org/medicare/report/how-much-is-enough-out-of-pocket-spending-among-medicare-beneficiaries-a-chartbook/

Murphy, Jody. "Century to Nix Retirees' Insurance Benefits." *Parkersburg News and Sentinel*, October 23, 2009.

Ruben, Mike. "Court to Rule on Century Benefit Reductions Plans." WOWK-TV News, November 17, 2009.

Rubin, Leslie. "Century Retirees to Lose Benefits." WCHS ABC 8, November 5, 2010.

WOWK-TV News. "Century Aluminum Executives Discuss Third Quarter Earnings Statement." October 28, 2010.

WOWK-TV News. "A High Price to Pay." November 17, 2010.

You Need to Fight

Karen recounted the stories involving her, including meeting Bryce Turner and the events leading to her decision to quit both jobs. Karen's daughter, Jodi, contributed details on the events that involved her. The details about Bryce Turner's life came from a document Bryce wrote outlining his fight with cancer and his loss of insurance. The article that resulted from the retirees' meeting is listed here.

Peterson, Erica. "Century Aluminum Retirees to Lose Health Insurance Jan. 1." West Virginia Public Broadcasting, November 12, 2010.

Civic Duty

Karen shared printed copies of the emails quoted or referenced in this chapter, including the emails she sent to Senators Rockefeller's and Manchin's offices. Karen recounted the meeting she organized, how the retirees began to work together, and the specific conversations she had with Sherry Breeden and Wes Holden. Wes and Sherry also provided additional details about these conversations. Jim Weltner, Les Shockey, and John Morris spoke about their early involvement writing letters and contacting their representatives. Some of these letters were shared with me by Karen.

Associated Press. "Retirees Rage as Century Ends Health Care Coverage." *Register-Herald*, November 12, 2010.

Hunt, Jared. "Century Says Health Care Coverage Cut Helped Profits." *Charleston Gazette-Mail*, May 4, 2011.

Nyden, Paul. "Century Aluminum Retirees Prepare for Benefits Meeting." *Charleston Gazette-Mail*, January 18, 2011.

Chapter Three

Epigraph

Karen Gorrell, email to West Virginia governor Joe Manchin, November 2010.

Choices

Jim Weltner shared the details about his life and career at the plant, including his early retirement, and his early involvement with the retirees' campaign. He, Karen, and Les Shockey recounted the meeting on February 14 and the circumstances surrounding the correspondence with Capito's office and the Employee Benefits Security Administration ruling. Les Shockey provided a copy of the letter from Capito. Details about Sam's life came from his obituary, from news coverage of the settlement, a written statement he wrote, and my conversation with Ann McKinney. Karen discussed the effect Sam's death had on her in multiple interviews. The reference to the number of deaths attributed to lack of insurance comes from Jess Mancini's article.

Associated Press. "Rockefeller Presses for Health Benefits." *Charleston Gazette-Mail*, February 25, 2011.

Associated Press. "Help Sought for W.Va's Century Aluminum Retirees." *Forbes*, February 25, 2011.

Baughan, Jeff. "Widow of Century Aluminum Retiree Shares Her Story." *Parkersburg News and Sentinel*, February 15, 2017.

Mancini, Jess. "Study: Death by Lack of Insurance." *Parkersburg News and Sentinel*, June 22, 2012.

Court Date

Karen provided copies of the emails quoted or referenced and recounted her decision to show up at Century's meeting at the courthouse as well as the events during the meeting and afterward. Ron and Betty Dixon also contributed details about this day. News articles about the the bill, cited in the next section (A Moral Issue) also informed my writing, while the articles here provide context for Century's case to lower its tax bill.

Karmasek, Jessica M. "Century Aluminum Loses Property Tax Appeal in W.Va. SC." *West Virginia Record*, June 6, 2012.

Ruben, Mike. "Century, AEP Pleased with 'Power Bill' Passage." WOWK-TV, March 11, 2010.

Stephens, Chris. "Century Aluminum Wants Plant Value Reduced $49.6 Million for Tax Purposes." *Jackson Newspapers*, September 7, 2010.

A Moral Issue

Details about the Capitol were informed by my visits and a description of the complex on the West Virginia Archives website. Karen shared copies of the emails referenced, including those written by Les Shockey and Bryce Turner. She also recounted the story of her conversation with Facemyer on the Capitol steps. The events leading up to and during the retirees' event in Charleston, including Facemyer's stance on the issue, were reported by local news sources, listed here. Karen also shared flyers, photos, and a copy of notes from her speech, which provided additional context. The article quoting Karen saying "Logan Kruger and Century Aluminum can kiss our hind end" was written by Jared Hunt (March 4, 2011).

Associated Press. "Century Aluminum Retirees Gather at W.Va. Capitol." *Forbes*, March 4, 2011.

Baucher, Todd. "Making Their Case." WTAP News, March 22, 2011.

Hunt, Jared. "Century Retirees Rally for Health Benefits." *Charleston Gazette-Mail*, March 4, 2011.

Hunt, Jared. ". . . Incentive Bill Fails." *Charleston Gazette-Mail*. March 3, 2011.

Nyden, Paul. "Workers Want Health-Care Benefits Restored." *Charleston Gazette-Mail*, March 4, 2011.

Peterson, Erica. "Century Retirees Rally at the Capitol to Protest Lost Health Care." West Virginia Public Broadcasting, March 4, 2011.

Saulton, Jeffrey. "Century Proposal Fails in Committee." *Parkersburg News and Sentinel*, March 2, 2011.

WV Metro News. "Century Aluminum Officials to Regroup." March 2, 2011.

WV Metro News. "Century Retirees Hoping for Good News." March 3, 2011.

WV Metro News. "A Possible Roadblock for Century Aluminum." March 1, 2011.

It's Not Us

The *Charleston Gazette-Mail* article that mentions the union's stance on the Century bill was "Senators' Attempt to Revive Century Bill Blocked" by Jared Hunt (March 3, 2011). Karen recounted the story about the "retirees coming after you themselves" and the details of her exchange with Leo Gerard and other union members, which were also captured in emails. She, John Morris, and Les Shockey contributed to my understanding of the retirees' perceptions of Steelworkers Organization for Active Retirees. News articles and the 2017 court settlement document were used to confirm the timeline of events related to the United Steelworkers (USW) court case. The following sources also provided context.

Hunt, Jared. "Senators' Attempt to Revive Century Bill Blocked." *Charleston Gazette-Mail*, March 3, 2011.

Ruben, Mike. "Court to Rule on Century Benefit Reductions Plans." WOWK-TV News, November 17, 2009.

Chapter Four

Epigraph

Karen Gorrell, email to retirees, April 2011.

Chagrin

Karen Gorrell, Les Shockey, John Morris, and Ripcord and Betty Dixon contributed to the story of the retirees' trip to Cleveland and their picket in front of John O'Brien's home. Karen provided a copy of a *Forbes* profile of O'Brien listing his salary. The news article published about this trip is listed. Any emails referenced were provided by Karen, including those detailing the challenges or circumstances of individual retirees. (Some of these details were also reported in news sources cited throughout the book.) Last names of these individuals have been omitted.

Christian, Barbara. "Retirees Protest Loss of Health Care Benefits." *Chagrin Valley Times*, April 7, 2011.

Early Retiree Reinsurance Program

Karen recounted her conversation with Bryce Turner about the Early Retiree Reinsurance Program (ERRP), her conversation with the benefits department at Century, and her efforts to make sense of the retirees' situation and seek assistance and guidance from their elected officials. I reviewed the ERRP website and fact sheets listed here in addition to the news articles listed. Details about the percentages of employers offering retiree insurance came from the Kaiser Family Foundation. Karen provided a flyer for the prayer vigil. Wes Holden, with Senator Rockefeller's office, contributed to the details of Rockefeller's early years in West Virginia, which are also recorded in a brief biography of Rockefeller on West Virginia University's West Virginia and Regional History Center website. Several press releases from Rockefeller's office and correspondence between Karen and the offices of her elected officials regarding the ERRP were also used as reference. The details about Mother Jones were informed by her autobiography and the AP article listed.

Associated Press. "Death Calls 'Mother' Jones, 100, Famous for Two Generations as Defender of Weak and Oppressed." *Milwaukee Leader*, December 1, 1910.

Centers for Medicare & Medicaid Services. "Early Retiree Reinsurance Program." https://www.cms.gov/marketplace/employers-sponsors/early-retiree-reinsurance-program

Claxton, Gary, Bianca DiJulio, Benjamin Finder, Janet Lundy, Megan McHugh, Awo Ose-Anto, Heidi Whitmore, Jeremy Pickreign, and Jon Gabel. "Employer Health Benefits Annual Survey." *Kaiser Family Foundation*, 2010. https://www.kff.org/wp-content/uploads/2013/04/8085.pdf

Heilprin, John. "Financier Marc Rich Dies in Switzerland." *San Diego Union-Tribune*, June 26, 2013.

Hunt, Jared. "Century Aluminum Retirees Picket for Health Care Benefits." *Charleston Gazette-Mail*, July 1, 2011.

Hunt, Jared. "Eliminating Benefits Boosts Century's Profits." *Charleston Daily Mail*, July 27, 2011.

Peterson, Erica. "Century Aluminum Retirees to Lose Health Insurance Jan. 1." West Virginia Public Broadcasting, November 12, 2010.

White House Office of the Press Secretary. "Fact Sheet: The Early Retiree Reinsurance Program." Washington, DC, May 4, 2010. https://obamawhitehouse.archives.gov/the-press-office/fact-sheet-early-retiree-reinsurance-program

WOWK-TV. "Rockefeller Asks Century Aluminum to Reconsider." December 8, 2010.

Shame on You

Karen, Ripcord and Betty Dixon, and John Morris provided an account of the visit to California and the planning leading up to it. Karen spoke about her husband's decision not to attend, and her children also contributed details about their family.

Karen explained the decision to open a checking account and form the Retiree Committee. She shared artifacts from the trip to California including receipts, the meeting invitation, a copy of the T-shirt design with Bryce Turner's headshot, emails to Mike Dildine and others at Century, and a photo album from the trip. John Morris, Les Shockey, Ripcord, and Betty Dixon all shared details about their lives.

Chapter Five

Epigraph

Karen Gorrell, email to Greg May, USW Local 14200, August 2011.

Promises

The *American Metal Market* article and *Charleston Gazette-Mail* articles referenced in the first paragraphs are listed here, along with articles detailing Governor Tomblin's commitment to supporting the retirees after meeting with them. Karen also recounted details about the retirees' meeting with the governor. Karen provided her correspondence with the West Virginia Attorney General's Office and other law firms about the potential for a class action suit, and this was also referenced in news articles. Karen provided copies of correspondence and press releases from elected officials related to their actions in regard to the ERRP, and a copy of the email she sent to retirees announcing the extension of coverage. Wes Holden contributed information about the efforts of Senator Rockefeller's office.

Hunt, Jared. "Century Aluminum Retirees Picket for Health Care Benefits." *Charleston Gazette-Mail*, July 1, 2011.

Hunt, Jared. "Century Retirees Finally Get to Meet with Tomblin." *Charleston Gazette-Mail*, June 22, 2011.

Hunt, Jared. "Century Talks to Include Retiree Benefits." *Charleston Gazette-Mail,* June 23, 2011.
Hunt, Jared. "Eliminating Benefits Boosts Century's Profits." *Charleston Daily Mail,* July 27, 2011.
Riley, Anne. "Rumors of Century Ravenswood Sale Mount." *American Metal Market,* June 22, 2011.
Tarr, Rachel. "Century Aluminum Sale." WVHS-TV Eyewitness Local News, June 27, 2011.
"Rockefeller Asks Century Aluminum to Reconsider." WOWK-TV, December 8, 2010.

Fort Unity

Karen described the effort that went into preparing for the Fort Unity rally and provided copies of the checks and notes that were sent as donations as well as copies of some of the flyers and emails she created. She shared a photo album of the rally, as did John Beaver, who also added details that informed the description of the rally. Karen recounted her phone conversation with Jim Centner, the subsequent meeting with retirees at a McDonald's, and her final visit with Bryce Turner. Ripcord and Jim Weltner also spoke about the conversation between Karen and Centner and the meeting that followed. Karen discussed her frustration at the court hearing and her lack of faith in the courts. A transcript of the audio recording of the court hearing was referenced. Any emails quoted or referenced were provided by Karen. The comment by Attorney General McGraw was captured by Todd Baucher for WTAP.

Baucher, Todd. "Fighting Back." WTAP News, August 27, 2011.
Nyden, Paul. "Century Retirees Plan Event to Fight Health Coverage Loss." *Charleston Gazette-Mail,* August 25, 2011.
Thomas, Landon, Jr. "Maker of OcyContin Reaches Settlement with West Virginia." *New York Times,* November 6, 2004.

WPWL-TV. "Former Century Aluminum Retirees Rally in Jackson County." West Virginia Media, August 27, 2011.

Washington

Karen shared the Alliance for Retired Americans (ARA) conference flyer, receipts for the retirees' travel, a copy of the handbill created for the ARA event, and the email correspondence she had engaged in when she was prepared to have a speaking role at the conference. She recounted the day that she learned she would not be speaking at the event, her decision to attend anyway, and the events that took place at the hotel, including her meeting the retiree from Marietta, and her conversations with Ripcord, Senator Manchin's office, and Jim Centner. Ripcord and Betty Dixon also contributed details about the trip to Washington DC, including the confrontation that took place in the hotel lobby.

Chapter Six

Epigraph

Karen Gorrell, email to retirees and supporters, March 2011.

Departure

Karen recounted her reaction to hearing about Kruger's departure and the events that followed. The news articles discussing Kruger's departure and the plant reopening are listed here, as are sources related to the Occupy movement and CEO compensation.

Bivens, Josh, and Jori Kandra. "CEO Pay Slightly Declined in 2022: But It Has Soared 1,209.2% since 1978 Compared with a 15.3% Rise in Typical Workers' Pay." Economic Policy Institute, 2023. https://www.epi.org/publication/ceo-pay-in-2022/

Century Aluminum. Press Release: "Century Aluminum Names Michael Bless as Acting President and Chief Executive Officer." Marketwire, November 15, 2011.

Gautney, Heather. "What Is Occupy Wall Street? The History of Leaderless Movements." *Washington Post*, October 10, 2011.

Hunt, Jared. "Retirees Celebrate Century Aluminum CEOs Resignation." *Charleston Gazette-Mail*. November 17, 2011.

Hunt, Jared. "Rumors Swirl around Century Aluminum Reopening." *Charleston Gazette-Mail*, December 19, 2011.

Nyden, P. "Century Aluminum Retirees Picket over Lost Benefits." *Charleston Gazette-Mail*, November 15, 2011.

Schneider, Nathan. "Occupy Wall Street: FAQ." *The Nation*, September 29, 2011.

Schultz, Ellen. *Retirement Heist: How Companies Plunder and Profit from the Nest Eggs of American Workers*. New York: Portfolio/Penguin, 2011.

Vaporean, C. "Century Aluminum Ex-CEO Says He Was Forced Out." Reuters, November 18, 2011.

Waite, S. "Former Century Exec Claims He Was Involuntarily Ousted." *American Metal Market*, November 21, 2011.

Occupied

Descriptions of the Occupy camp were shared by Karen Gorrell, Chad Gorrell, Hoot Gibson, Bill Stephens, Ripcord and Betty Dixon, and others. Karen recounted the day she proposed the idea to the retirees and the day she learned about Sonny's stroke. Chad Gorrell recounted his experience visiting camp and afterward. Karen's personal Facebook page and the Occupy Century Aluminum Facebook page, maintained by Karen, informed the writing of this chapter. I also referenced photos, including several taken by James Fassinger.

Gerard, Leo. "Retirees Occupy Century Aluminum." *Truthout*, January 30, 2012.

Matics, Dan. "Century Retirees Ring in New Year." WCHS-TV: Eyewitness News Online, December 31, 2011.
Saulton, Jeffrey. "Movement Staged by Century Retirees." *Parkersburg News and Sentinel,* December 26, 2011.

Negotiations

Les Shockey, John Morris, and Ripcord spoke about John Hoerner's visits to Ravenswood. Karen recounted her conversations with John Hoerner and Century's lawyer and her disapproval of the proposal. She and John Beaver shared details about the negotiation meeting. John also shared additional details about his life and his decision to attend the meeting. News of Bless becoming CEO was announced by Century Aluminum. My interview with Bless informed my writing about him and his meeting with retirees at the Occupy camp. Karen and Ripcord also recounted meeting Bless for the first time at camp. Information about Bless's annual compensation came from a Forbes profile. Karen's speech at the Occupy site was captured in a video recorded by James Fassinger. I also referenced the Occupy Century Aluminum Facebook page, maintained by Karen, which documented visits by the USW, Governor Tomblin, and others.

Adkins, Roger. "Constellium Cuts Ribbon on $46 Million Stretcher." *Jackson Newspapers,* January 24, 2012.
Nyden, Hunt. "Century Retirees Talk with Company Officials." *Charleston Gazette-Mail,* January 26, 2012.
Waite, Suzy. "Century W.Va. Retirees Resume Talks." *American Metal Market,* January 30, 2012.

Chapter Seven

Epigraph

Karen Gorrell, email to the Public Service Commission (PSC) of West Virginia, June 2012.

Deal

Karen recounted her attempt to drum up support leading into the negotiation meeting in Charleston and shared details about the protests that took place at multiple locations. She shared photos from some of these events. Karen, Hoot Gibson, Jim Weltner, and Ripcord contributed to the story of Hoot returning forty dollars to John Hoerner and Hoerner's multiple visits to the camp. The news articles mentioned or quoted regarding the settlement are listed here. Press releases from Rockefeller and Manchin, a recording of Rockefeller's senate speech, the Occupy Century Aluminum Facebook page, Karen's Facebook page, a summary of the 2012 settlement agreement, and photos of the Occupy camp also were referenced in writing this chapter. Hoot and Karen Gorrell shared details about the last day at camp. Karen described the meeting with the voluntary employees' beneficiary association (VEBA) administrators before the retirees' vote, her distress, and the phone calls she made to Raamie Barker.

Century Aluminum. Press Release: "Michael Bless Named Chief Executive Officer of Century Aluminum." February 7, 2012. https://centuryaluminum.com/investors/press-releases/press-release-details/2012/Michael-Bless-Named-Chief-Executive-Officer-of-Century-Aluminum/default.aspx

Hunt, Jared. "Century Aluminum Retirees Reach Common Ground." *Charleston Gazette-Mail*, February 29, 2012.

Hunt, Jared. "Century May Restore Benefits." *Charleston Gazette-Mail*, February 27, 2012.

Kaull, April. "Century Aluminum, Retirees Could Be Close to a Deal; May Pave the Way to Restart Plant." WOWK-TV, February 29, 2012.

Nyden, Paul. "Century Aluminum Retirees Vote to Accept Benefits Settlement." *Charleston Gazette-Mail*, March 15, 2012.

Nyden, Paul. "Century Retirees to Vote on Offer Thursday." *Charleston Gazette-Mail*, March 11, 2012.

Nyden, Paul. "High Hopes in Ravenswood." *Charleston Gazette-Mail*, February 29, 2012.

Nyden, Paul. "Rockefeller, Manchin Praise Century Retirees' Effort." *Charleston Gazette-Mail*, March 14, 2012.

Office of Senator John D. Rockefeller. "Rockefeller Calls Final Century Aluminum Deal Great News for Workers and Retirees." Press Release, March 2, 2012.

Power

Karen, John Morris, and Les Shockey recounted the retirees' visit to the Capitol for the bill's vote, and their gratitude to the legislature for its support. Karen shared several photos from this trip and of the bill's signing at the plant. News coverage on these events, including articles discussing the economic impact of the plant closing, are listed here. The reference to electricity costs at the plant comes from Ruben's "Century, AEP Pleased with Power Bill Passage." There was extensive news coverage of the negotiations between Century and the Appalachian Power Company (APCo), and the PSC hearings. Paul Nyden (March 14, 2012) reported on the unemployment rate since the recession, including the record-low employment in manufacturing. Karen shared the letter she wrote to the PSC and described the meeting the retirees had with Mike Bless to discuss their concerns (also reported by Paul Nyden on July 10, 2012). Karen described why she had changed her decision and opted not to support the proposal in multiple interviews. "Let's get that plant open and let's join hands and let's stand together and watch that parking lot fill back up" was originally quoted by Jared Hunt (August 1, 2012), while "They have dangled health care benefits and restoration of lost jobs in front of the retirees and the state like a piece of meat—just beyond our reach" and "We are sorry to say that even though we have faced many roadblocks along the way, that Century's recent decision felt like a knockout punch" both were quoted by Paul Fallon (October 12, 2012).

Ali, Ann. "Century Aluminum Hopes to Reopen Plant but Wants Appalachian Power Customers to Help Pay the Bill." *State Journal*, June 7, 2012.

Ali, Ann. "Century Retirees Caught in the Middle of Plant Opening." *State Journal*, June 7, 2012.

Fallon, Paul. "Century Retirees Feel Betrayed by Decision." *Charleston Daily Mail*, October 12, 2012.

Hohmann, George. "Century Needs Comfort Margin to Restart." *Charleston Gazette-Mail*, May 18, 2012.

Hohmann, George. "Century's Difficult Timing." *Charleston Gazette-Mail*, May 20, 2012.

Hohmann, George. "Group Sympathetic to Century Requests for Rate Hike." *Charleston Gazette-Mail*, May 16, 2012.

Hohmann, George. "PSC Consumer Advocate Weighs In on Century Rate Plan." *Charleston Gazette-Mail*, May 17, 2012.

Hohmann, George. "Steel Company Exec Urges a Better WV Business Climate." *Charleston Gazette-Mail*, September 2, 2012.

Hohmann, George. "Utility Seeks Recovery of Past Century Deficit." *Charleston Daily Mail*, May 17, 2012.

Hunt, Jared. "Aluminum Prices Sharply Up." *Charleston Gazette-Mail*, September 18, 2012.

Hunt, Jared. "Another Proposal Created in Century Case." *Charleston Gazette-Mail*, August 21, 2012.

Hunt, Jared. "Appalachian Power Counters Century's Re-Start Plan." *Charleston Gazette-Mail*, August 1, 2012.

Hunt, Jared. "Attorney Urges Rejection of Century Rate Proposal." *Charleston Gazette-Mail*, July 31, 2012.

Hunt, Jared. "Century Alters Its Rate Proposal." *Charleston Gazette-Mail*, July 24, 2012.

Hunt, Jared. "Century Aluminum Won't Restart Plant under Current Conditions." *Charleston Daily Mail,* October 9, 2012.

Hunt, Jared. "Century Chief Says Progress Made on Plant." *Charleston Gazette-Mail,* April 27, 2012.

Hunt, Jared. "Century on Track to Reopen by Fall." *Charleston Gazette-Mail,* March 29, 2012.

Hunt, Jared. "Century Still Reviewing PSC Ruling on Power Rate Structure." *Charleston Gazette-Mail,* October 5, 2012.

Hunt, Jared. "Chairman Requests Rate Plan Counterproposal from Appalachian Power." *Charleston Gazette-Mail,* August 1, 2012.

Hunt, Jared. "Commission Gives Century More Time to Appeal Rate." *Charleston Gazette-Mail,* October 10, 2012.

Hunt, Jared. "Commission Pushes Back Decision on Power Rate." *Charleston Gazette-Mail,* August 13, 2012.

Hunt, Jared. "Effect of Electric Rate on Customers Uncertain." *Charleston Gazette-Mail,* May 16, 2012.

Hunt, Jared. "Final Century Rate Proposals Submitted to PSC." *Charleston Gazette-Mail,* August 30, 2012.

Hunt, Jared. "Hearing to Begin on Century Proposal." *Charleston Gazette-Mail,* July 30, 2012.

Hunt, Jared. "Official Worried over Century Rate Plan." *Charleston Gazette-Mail,* June 7, 2012.

Hunt, Jared. "PSC Seeking Details on Century Aluminum Counter-Proposal." *Charleston Daily Mail,* September 25, 2012.

Hunt, Jared. "Retirees Back Century Rate." *Charleston Daily Mail,* June 1, 2012.

Hunt, Jared. "State Supreme Court Rejects Century Plant Tax Reduction." *Charleston Daily Mail,* May 30, 2012.

Kersey, Lori. "Century Attorney: Proposed Rate Change Might Not Affect Average Customer." *Charleston Gazette-Mail,* August 6, 2012.

Kersey, Lori. "Consumer Advocate: Century Would Profit at Ratepayer Expense." *Charleston Gazette-Mail,* August 28, 2012.

Kersey, Lori. "PSC: Century Aluminum Will Have until Oct. 26 to File Petition." *Charleston Gazette-Mail,* October 11, 2012.

Kersey, Lori. "PSC: Century's Special Rate Can't Put Other Power Customers at Risk." *Charleston Gazette-Mail,* October 4, 2012.

Kuykendall, Taylor. "Ravenswood: Century Plant 'Doesn't Define Us.'" *State Journal,* May 9, 2013.

Messina, Lawrence. "After Fight, Century Retirees Mark Victory." *Charleston Gazette-Mail,* March 18, 2012.

Nyden, Paul. "Century Retiree Leader Talks about Meeting with CEO." *Charleston Gazette-Mail,* July 10, 2012.

Nyden, Paul. "Century Says PSC Offer Not Enough to Restart Ravenswood Plant." *Charleston Gazette-Mail,* October 9, 2012.

Nyden, Paul. "Government, Coal Employment Up; Manufacturing Jobs See Dramatic Drop." *Charleston Gazette-Mail,* March 14, 2012.

Nyden, Paul. "Leader for Century Aluminum Retirees Raises New Concerns in Letter." *Charleston Gazette-Mail,* June 12, 2012.

Nyden, Paul. "PSC: Century, Appalachian Power Fail to Reach Agreement." *Charleston Gazette-Mail,* May 12, 2012.

Nyden, Paul. "PSC Wraps Up Healings on Century Rate." *Charleston Gazette-Mail,* August 1, 2012.

Nyden, Paul. "Rockefeller Urges Century CEO to Restore Health Benefits." *Charleston Gazette-Mail,* June 30, 2012.

Nyden, Paul. "Utility Deal's Approval Key to Reopening Aluminum Plant." *Charleston Gazette-Mail,* April 24, 2012.

Office of Senator John D. Rockefeller. "Rockefeller Calls Final Century Aluminum Deal Great News for Workers and Retirees." Press Release, March 2, 2012.

Parkersburg News and Sentinel. "Century Plant Reopening Delayed." May 13, 2012.

PSC. "PSC Sets Special Rate for Century Aluminum but Refuses to Place Additional Risk on APCo Customers." Press Release, October 4, 2012.

"Representative for Retirees Blasts Century." *Charleston Gazette-Mail,* October 11, 2012.

Ruben, Mike. "Century, AEP Pleased with Power Bill Passage." Century Aluminum WV, March 11, 2010.

SHADAC. "The Opioid Epidemic in the United States." Accessed December 23, 2024. https://www.shadac.org/opioid-epidemic-united-states

Vaporean, Carole. "Century Enters Power Talks in Bid to Restart Smelter." Reuters, March 23, 2012.

Workman, Megan. "Century Plan Called 'Absurd, Ridiculous, Risky.'" *Charleston Gazette-Mail,* October 27, 2012.

Workman, Megan. "Century Says No to Counter-Proposal on Rate Request." *Charleston Gazette-Mail,* August 22, 2012.

Workman, Megan. "Century to PSC: Reconsider Electricity Ruling." *Charleston Gazette-Mail,* October 26, 2012.

You Decide

The description of Hawesville was informed by my conversations with John Beaver and the article listed here. Karen recounted her encounter with the worker wearing a pin, and she, other retirees, and John Beaver described the events leading up to and during the Health Fair, including setting up the cemetery. Both Karen and John Beaver shared photos from the event. Karen recounted her conversation with the plant employee and her reflections on the lockout. Karen emphasized in multiple conversations that the retirees were respectful and nonviolent and discussed her decision not to allow other protesters to join their camp to minimize the risk of any incidents. I pulled from many conversations with Karen to address her reflections and approach to organizing.

Lawrence, Keith. "Hancock One of Nation's Most Industrialized Counties." *Messenger-Inquirer*, September 27, 2020.

Chapter Eight

Epigraph

Hunt, Jared. "Century Retirees to Protest at Ravenswood Plant." *Charleston Gazette-Mail*, March 6, 2013.

Respect

Most of the details from this chapter were constructed from the numerous news sources discussing Century's efforts to secure rates agreements for electricity in West Virginia and Kentucky. These are listed here. The article mentioning the $18 million saved by Century was titled "Century Plant Retiree Benefits at Risk." Karen shared the emails mentioned and discussed how the expiration of the settlement agreement had impacted her and how she, nevertheless, knew she couldn't walk away from her promise to Bryce. The retirees' travel logs submitted during the final settlement helped fill in details about their events. Jim Weltner shared details about his rising health costs in our conversation. The conversation between the retirees, Mike Bless, and Terrence Wilkinson in Chicago is documented in a video recorded by James Fassinger. Karen recounted her speech to the board and her reflection on the conversation with Wilkinson. In our conversation, John Morris shared his theories on why people in Chicago are so thin.

Ali, Ann. "Century Aluminum Power Rate Negotiations Resume in Ky." *State Journal*, March 2013.

Ali, Ann. "Century Aluminum to Get Ky. Power on Open Market, Acquire Sebree Smelter." *State Journal*, April 29, 2013.

Ali, Ann. "PSC Denies Rate Reconsideration Hearing in Century Case." *State Journal*, December 14, 2012.

Ali, Ann. "WV Waits for Action, Century Aluminum Completes Its Acquisition of Ky. Smelter." *State Journal*, June 3, 2013.

Associated Press. "Ky. Governor Urges Century Aluminum, Power Utility to Compromise." *Charleston Gazette-Mail*, February 24, 2013.

Associated Press. "Ky. Lawmakers Pull Bill to Aid Century Smelter." *Charleston Gazette-Mail*, March 10, 2013.

Associated Press. "Century Aluminum Reports First Quarter Profit." *Charleston Gazette-Mail*, April 25, 2013.

Associated Press. "Ky. Century Aluminum Smelter Gets Open Market Power Approval." *Charleston Gazette-Mail*, August 14, 2013.

Century Aluminum. Press Release: "Century Aluminum Announces Agreement to Acquire Sebree, KY Smelter." Globe News Wire, April 29, 2013. https://www.globenewswire.com/news-release/2013/04/29/542516/0/is/Century-Aluminum-Announces-Agreement-to-Acquire-Sebree-KY-Smelter.html

Century Aluminum. Press Release: "Century, Big Rivers and Kenergy Reach Tentative Agreement on Framework for Market Priced Power for Hawesville Smelter." Yahoo Finance, April 29, 2013. https://finance.yahoo.com/news/century-big-rivers-kenergy-reach-130000594.html

Hunt, Jared. "Aluminum Companies Play from Same Book." *Charleston Gazette-Mail*, October 14, 2013.

Hunt, Jared. "Century Maintains Commitment to Plant." *Charleston Gazette-Mail*, November 2, 2012.

Hunt, Jared. "Century Plant Retiree Benefits at Risk." *Charleston Gazette-Mail,* March 29, 2013.

Hunt, Jared. "Century Power Rate Talks at Early Stage." *Charleston Gazette-Mail,* March 4, 2013.

Hunt, Jared. "Century Retirees to Protest at Ravenswood Plant." *Charleston Gazette-Mail,* March 6, 2013.

Hunt, Jared. "Kentucky Does Very Little to Entice Century." *Charleston Gazette-Mail,* May 2, 2013.

Hunt, Jared. "PSC Denies Century Aluminum's Special Power Rate Request." *Charleston Gazette-Mail,* December 14, 2012.

Hunt, Jared. "Ravenswood Restart No Longer a Top Priority at Century." *Charleston Gazette-Mail,* July 30, 2013.

Kersey, Lori. "Century 'Committed' to Ravenswood Plant Restart." *Charleston Gazette-Mail,* December 17, 2012.

Kersey, Lori. "PSC to Address Reconsideration, Clarification Requests Dec. 14." *Charleston Gazette-Mail,* November 18, 2012.

Nyden, Paul. "Century Completes Purchase of Ky. Smelter." *Charleston Gazette-Mail,* June 3, 2013.

Nyden, Paul. "Ravenswood Idel, Century Buying Ky. Smelter." *Charleston Gazette-Mail,* April 29, 2013.

"'Occupy' Camp Returns to Century Aluminum." *USW@Work,* Volume 8-2 (2013): 31.

"Century Aluminum Retirees to Protest Facility." *Parkersburg News and Sentinel,* August 15, 2013.

"Century Aluminum Seeks Deal for Restart." *Parkersburg News and Sentinel,* April 2, 2013.

"Century Retirees to Protest Today." *Parkersburg News and Sentinel,* May 31, 2013.

Robbins, Lisa. "Century Aluminum Retirees Stage 24-Hour Protest in Jackson County." WOWK-TV, March 7, 2013.

Stinnett, Chuck. "Century Aluminum Warns of Possible Smelter Closure." *Evansville Courier and Press*, April 16, 2013.

Workman, Megan. "Century Says It's Committed to Reopening Ravenswood Plant." *Charleston Gazette-Mail*, February 21, 2013.

Workman, Megan. "PSC Denies Special Power Rate for Century Aluminum." *Charleston Gazette-Mail*, December 14, 2012.

Faith

Karen recounted the visit to Sebree, the gift of the Bible, and having Senator Rockefeller and Wes Holden to her house for dinner. The brief description of Sebree was informed by the article cited here. Karen also discussed Mike's growing concerns about her involvement in the campaign, and her children, Chad and Jodi, contributed details here as well. The cards mentioned were included in the scrapbooks Karen shared, except for the printed quote from Sherry Breeden, which Karen kept taped to her computer. Karen listed the unions that she had received donations from over the years and included copies of several checks the retirees received. In more than one conversation, Karen spoke of the outpouring of support that kept her inspired during difficult times.

Boyett, Frank. "Boyett: Local Aluminum Smelter Helped Keep Copper Company in Business." *Gleaner*, July 17, 2020.

Covered

Century's "commitment" to Ravenswood was reported in the November 4, 2013, *Charleston Gazette-Mail* article listed here. Karen recounted her decision not to enroll in the Affordable Care Act, and she and Wes Holden shared details related to the health scare after her TOPS (Taking Off Pounds Sensibly) meeting, Karen's doctor's visit, and the conversation the two of them had afterward. Karen shared her husband's reaction, and I expanded on this using context and details from my conversations with Karen and her children. Karen's children also contributed details about the emotional and physical toll of the campaign. Details regarding the Bankruptcy Protection Act, the United Mine Workers of America and Patriot Coal, and the purchase of the Mount Holly smelter were covered in the sources listed here and from Karen's Facebook posts. The article quoting Karen was written by Paul Nyden on December 1, 2014.

Charleston Gazette-Mail. "Century Aluminum Reports Net Loss." November 4, 2013.

Hunt, Jared. "Century Still Has Year-End Target for Ravenswood." *Charleston Gazette-Mail*, October 29, 2014.

Hunt, Jared. "Century Still Working for Ravenswood Plant Restart." *Charleston Gazette-Mail*, July 31, 2014.

Hunt, Jared. "Fortunes Improve for Century Aluminum." *Charleston Gazette-Mail*, September 4, 2014.

MacGillis, Alec. "The Incredible Disappearing Health Benefits." *Truthout*, February 19, 2013.

Maher, Kris. "Patriot Coal Seeks Trust to Limit Retiree Health Costs." *Wall Street Journal*, January 29, 2013.

Nyden, Paul. "Bill Introduced to Protect Miner Benefits." *Charleston Gazette-Mail*, August 2, 2013.

Nyden, Paul. "Ravenswood Retiree Leader Wonders about Century Purchase." *Charleston Gazette-Mail*, October 25, 2014.

Nyden, Paul. "Century Buys Smelter in South Carolina." *Charleston Gazette-Mail*, December 1, 2014.

"Legislation Takes Aim at Unfair Benefit Cuts." *Parkersburg News and Sentinel*, June 4, 2014.

"Senator Manchin's Work on Securing Miners' Pensions and Health Care." n.d. https://www.wdtv.com/content/news/Manchin-leads-effort-to-secure-miners-pensions-and-healthcare-566244501.html

Office of Senator Elizabeth Warren. "Rockefeller, Warren Introduce Legislation to Protect Employees and Retirees from Unfair Benefit Cuts." Press release, June 3, 2014.

Chapter Nine

Epigraph

Karen Gorrell, email to APCo CEO Charles Patton, June 2015.

Progress

Karen explained the addition of Hoot and Mel to the retiree committee and talked at length about her concerns over the 2012 settlement agreement in several of our conversations. She shared a copy of the letter the committee wrote to Century, her emails forwarding the letter to others, and the email exchange between her and Bless regarding Hawesville. News articles discussing the events in Ravenswood and Hawesville are included here. Karen discussed her outreach to the Hawesville union. Mike Bless mentioned his trip to Kentucky and contributed details about this labor dispute.

Associated Press. "Century Aluminum CO. Sends Lockout Notice to Union Local." *Owensboro Messenger-Inquirer*, May 2, 2015.

Associated Press. "Century Aluminum Locks Union Workers Out of Ky. Plant." *Charleston Gazette-Mail*, May 12, 2015.

Cohen, Luc. "Century Aluminum Braces for Kentucky Lockout as USW Reject Deal." Reuters, May 5, 2015.

Craig, Berry. "Gilded Age Union Busting." LA Progressive, May 16, 2015. https://www.laprogressive.com/labor-social-justice/united-steelworkers

Haas, Richard, and Tony Montana. "USW Stands for Order in Chaos Created by Century Aluminum." USW Blog, May 21, 2015. https://usw.org/news/usw-stands-for-order-in-chaos-created-by-century-aluminum/

Hunt, Jared. "APCo's Hands Tied on Century Proposal." *Charleston Gazette-Mail*, May 14, 2015.

Hunt, Jared. "Century Aluminum in Talks over New Ravenswood Power Rate Plan." *Charleston Gazette-Mail*, February 24, 2015.

Hunt, Jared. "Century May Drop Ravenswood Restart Effort." *Charleston Gazette-Mail*, April 30, 2015.

Lawrence, Chris. "Charting Century's Next Move." WV MetroNews, May 1, 2015.

Matyi, Bob. "Century Aluminum Hiring Temporary Replacement Workers for Smelter: USW." *Platts News*, May 20, 2015.

Monroe, Jackie. "Contract Negotiations Fail between Century Aluminum and Union Employees." 14News, May 4, 2015.

"Century Aluminum Claims Picketers Creating Unsafe Environment." Nexstar Broadcasting, May 20, 2015.

"Lockout Begins at Century Aluminum Plant in Hancock County." Nexstar Broadcasting, May 12, 2015.

Parker, T. J. "Century Aluminum Workers Planning Demonstration." 14News, April 29, 2015.

"FMCS Statement on Tentative Settlement between United Steelworkers Local 9423 and Century Aluminum Co. in Kentucky." PRNewswire, June 9, 2015.

"BRIEF-USW to Vote on Century Aluminum's Final Offer at Kentucky Smelter." Reuters, April 29, 2015.

Ross, Jim. "Century Aluminum Still in Talks to Re-Open Ravenswood, WV Plant." *State Journal*, May 4, 2015.

Rowe, Jordan. "Century Aluminum Officials 'Disappointed' by Employees Rejection of Contract Offer." 14News, May 5, 2015.

Rowe, Jordan. "Tentative Agreement Reached between Century Aluminum, Union." 14News, June 9, 2015.

Stinnett, Chuck. "Century Hawesville Workers Reject Final Offer, Face Lockout Monday." Journal Media Group, May 5, 2015.

USW. "Century Aluminum Locks Out 560 Steelworker at Kentucky Smelter." PR Newswire, May 12, 2015. https:www.prnewswire.com/news-releases/century-aluminum-locks-out-560-steelworkers-at-kentucky-smelter-3000081846.html

Yam, Polly. "Century Aluminum US Plant Lockout in Prospect after Union Rejects Deal." Reuters, May 12, 2015.

On to Ravenswood!

Karen shared the emails mentioned or quoted and provided a copy of the letter she wrote to Patton. Karen recounted her car accident and visit to the ER. The health conditions of retirees were shared by Karen as testimony she had collected or in interviews with retirees, or they were included as testimony in court documents. Karen and her daughter both shared details about Jodi's wedding. Chad Gorrell shared details about his back surgery and about his family. Karen, Mike Bless, and John Morris contributed details about the retirees meeting with Bless in Charleston.

Aluminum's End

News sources discussing the plant closure, the Hawesville closure, and the outlook for the aluminum industry are listed here. Emails and press releases from Caputo and Manchin were shared by

Karen. She also recounted her experience in Chicago and how she came to believe that her message had gotten through to the board. Mike Bless contributed to the description of the board meeting. Details about the judge's ruling in the case came from the 2017 settlement documents. In multiple conversations, Karen explained how she maintained faith in Bless despite others' hesitations and that the two of them came to respect one another.

Ali, Ann. "Century Aluminum Permanently Closes Ravenswood, WV Plant." *State Journal*, July 27, 2015.

"Editorial: A Sad End to Century's Ravenswood Smelter." *Charleston Gazette-Mail*, July 29, 2015.

Home, Andy. "Is the Curtain Coming Down on US Aluminum Smelting?" Reuters, November 24, 2015.

Lannon, Andrea. "Century Aluminum Closes Ravenswood Plant." *Charleston Gazette-Mail*, July 28, 2015.

Lawrence, Chris. "Power Costs, Aluminum Pricing Sink Century Plant." WV MetroNews, July 28, 2015.

Lawrence, Keith. "Century Aluminum to Temporarily Close Hawesville Smelter." *Owensboro Messenger-Inquirer*, August 25, 2015

Nyden, Paul. "Century Aluminum Closes Its Doors for Good." *Charleston Gazette-Mail*, August 2, 2015.

Nyden, Paul. "Officials: Century Closure a Disappointment for Ravenswood." *Charleston Gazette-Mail*, July 28, 2015.

"UPDATE: Permanent Closure of Century Aluminum Sparks Domino Effect." WSAZ News, July 28, 2015.

Chapter Ten

Epigraph

Karen Gorrell, email to Century Aluminum CEO Mike Bless, September 2015.

Settled

Karen recounted receiving the email from Bless, their meeting in Charleston, and the delays in scheduling the official negotiations meeting. My conversation with Bless also informed this section. Karen recounted her call to Tom Conway, how she felt during the meeting with the USW before negotiations, and the events after that meeting. Details of the settlement, including dates, were informed by a copy of the settlement agreement and the announcement letter sent to retirees. The newspapers announcing the settlement agreement are listed here. The article that mentions Copenhaver calling the settlement "generous" is titled "Judge Approves $23M Settlement for Century Aluminum Employees," by Lacie Pierson. Emails mentioned or quoted were shared by Karen, including emails discussing the work of verifying retiree addresses and her emails to the trust administrators.

Ali, Ann. "Century Retirees Mark Emotional Health Care Settlement." *State Journal*, February 18, 2017.

Ali, Ann. "Editorial: Century Aluminum Settles Retiree Story the Right Way." *State Journal*, February 20, 2017.

"Century Aluminum Agrees to Fund Health Care Benefits for Retirees." USW@Work, Volume 12/2 (Spring 2017).

"Century Aluminum Settles with Retirees over Health Care Benefits." *Charleston Gazette-Mail*, February 14, 2017.

"Century to Fund Health Benefits for Retirees." *Charleston Gazette-Mail*, February 11, 2017.

"Century Aluminum Retirees Celebrate Pending Return of Health Benefits." *Parkersburg News and Sentinel*, February 15, 2017.

"Judge OKs Century Aluminum Retiree Settlement." *Parkersburg News and Sentinel*, August 16, 2017.

Pierson, Lacie. "Judge Approves $23M Settlement for Century Aluminum Employees." *Charleston Gazette-Mail*, August 14, 2017.

Insured

Karen shared a copy of the travel log she submitted for reimbursement and the checks she and Mike received. The reimbursement for the Retiree Committee was outlined in the settlement agreement. The events at the retiree meeting and the meeting with students were recorded and transcribed by me. Karen contributed additional context about how she felt about those events, and about the events leading up to and after receiving her first payments from the VEBA trust.

"Century to Fund Health Benefits for Retirees." *Charleston Gazette-Mail*, February 11, 2017.

"Picnic to Celebrate Century Aluminum Benefits Settlement." *Parkersburg News and Sentinel*, October 2, 2017.

Epilogue

Epigraph

Wes Holden, director of constituent services for Senator Jay Rockefeller, interview with the author, 2018.

About the Author

Julia Flint is a writer from Northern Appalachia. With a background in qualitative research, she has worked as a research assistant for education and community health projects and as an instructor with the Ohio University Global Health Initiative. She currently lives in Pittsburgh, Pennsylvania.